JESUS IN (WHAT?) CONTEXT

MINDI JO FURBY

First published 2023
ISBN: 978-1-943413-13-3

Visit us on the web!
www.mindijofurby.com
Published by: KingsWynd Books
www.kingswynd.com
KingsWynd exists to fight biblical illiteracy in our families, church, communities, and world. Our goal is to help others love God and become more like Jesus through His Word. We accomplish this through publishing books, articles, curriculum, and Bible studies used by individuals and churches throughout the world.
For more information about KingsWynd Books, visit www.kingswynd.com.

Scripture, unless otherwise noted, taken from the NEW AMERICAN STANDARD BIBLE®, Copyright© 1960, 1962, 1963, 1968, 1971, 1972, 1973, 1975, 1977, 1995 by The Lockman Foundation. Used by permission.
Author: Mindi Jo Furby
Edited by: Christina Miller
Cover by: Katie G. Turner
Formatting by: Polgarus Studio

Contents

Chapter One
The Issue

Archeology fascinates me. Relentlessly pursuing history through enormous, time-consuming digs—investing countless hours of backbreaking work in hopes of finding something (anything!) that will shed light on even a miniscule aspect of history…talk about dedication. Archeologists spend decades digging, evaluating, testing, and digging some more. Their devotion is astounding, and all for the sake of understanding history better—to have a more accurate, fully formed comprehension of ancient peoples and events.

Archeologists put Christians to shame. They spend years digging up and sifting through dirt and even more time evaluating what precious little they discover, putting it into historical context. Contrarily, many Christians barely spend fifteen minutes digging through the text on which they claim to base their lives and eternal destinies. We won't read beyond superficial interpretations of Scripture, so we're consequently "tossed here and there by waves and carried about by every wind of doctrine, by the trickery of men, by craftiness in deceitful scheming" (Ephesians 4:14). Because of our laziness and gross lack of dedication to truth, havoc is being wreaked on both micro (personal/familial) and macro (universal church/world) levels.

I first noticed this disturbing trend in college. One of my Bible classes was New Testament Backgrounds, which is akin to New Testament text archeology. The entire purpose of the class was to put the New Testament in historical context—to dig through history books and other sources to gauge what life was really like during the years Christ and the early church walked the earth. About halfway through the course, a particular lecture was dedicated to the crucifixion and exploring what happened and how. Did you know there were multiple cross shapes, not just the traditional "t"? Or that Jesus was so brutally beaten before getting to the cross, His insides were exposed through His back? Needless to say, it was an intense, almost excruciating hour, listening to my professor walk us through the disturbing details.

As I sat with tears in my eyes, contemplating how and why this perfect God-man would endure so much for such unworthy people, I glanced to my right and noticed a classmate hunched over on his desk…sleeping.

My distress over the crucifixion gave way to fuming anger that someone (in an elective class, no less) could sleep through such a topic. Did he not realize the weight of the subject—the enormous, eternal ramifications it bore—not only to his faith personally but to the church and world? How could he not care?

Another young man in another Bible class took a different approach. While discussing Judas's betrayal of Jesus as described in the book of John, this student posed a long, speculative theory about how Judas was probably coerced, pressured, or blackmailed into betraying Jesus. This student was opinionated on the matter and quite loud in his resolutions. Our professor patiently explained why the student's conclusions, though theoretically possible, were not a responsible way to conduct hermeneutics (how to interpret Scripture, more on that subject later). But the student kept arguing. I sat quietly until that point. But I was also taking a class on the gospel of Matthew and knew the student's theory was blatantly false. So, much to the relief of the professor, I raised my hand and calmly read Matthew 26:14–16:

> Then one of the twelve, named Judas Iscariot, went to the chief priests and said, "What are you willing to give me to betray Him to you?" And they weighed out thirty pieces of silver to him. From then on he began looking for a good opportunity to betray Jesus.

Judas was most certainly not a victim of blackmail or anything else. As you can imagine, the student promptly closed his mouth, shrank in his chair, and remained quiet the rest of the class. With the reading of just three verses, his whole argument fell apart, and he knew his wild, speculative theories had no basis in reality.

Unlike the first student, this student engaged with Scripture and spent time thinking through the text. However, he did not conduct his study responsibly, nor did he perform due diligence in his biblical excavations. He approached Scripture incorrectly, and while it may have been unintentional, he proved that he thought he stood in authority over Scripture, not the other way around.

While on opposite sides of the spectrum, both of these students represent a serious issue plaguing the church today— gross biblical illiteracy. Some, like the first student, simply don't care. They like the idea of going to heaven when they die, so they say a prayer to attain their "get out of hell free card," thinking they can cash it in when they approach the pearly gates. But any more dedication than that is an imposition on their lifestyles, and that's not what they signed up for.

Contrarily, the second student represents church members who are liberal in their approach to Scripture. They don't understand (either by ignorance or deliberate choice) how to read, interpret, and apply Scripture responsibly. Thus, they draw erroneous conclusions, warp theology, and inevitably lead others further from the truth of God's Word. Some want to be relevant to the world, desperately trying to conform Scripture to current culture climates so they don't seem offensive. Or maybe they just want to fit in. Others prefer a prosperity gospel and twist the Bible to justify their misaligned priorities. Regardless of motivation, this group cares far more about their agendas than they do the integrity of Scripture. Sadly, many don't realize what they're doing.

These experiences, among others, would become monumental in crafting my ministry purpose years later—to fight biblical illiteracy one publication at a time. I don't know these young men's stories, but it broke my heart to see students (proclaiming to be Christians) act so nonchalantly and irresponsibly regarding Scripture. And that got me thinking: if they—Christian students at a Christian university taking voluntary Bible classes—do not care enough even to stay awake and maintain the integrity of proper hermeneutics, how will regular church members? How will our children? And what on earth can I do to change it?

After finishing my master's degree, I began teaching hermeneutics classes (teaching people how to read, interpret, and apply Scripture correctly—again, like Bible text archeology). My hunger grew even more. Women who had grown up in church came to me after class, tears splashing on the carpet, asking me why no one had told them what the Bible really was or how they can study it for themselves. Cue my own tears.

So I began a ministry helping people do just that—become biblically literate.

Yet recently, I found myself becoming unsettled in an area I've never really cared about: politics. It blew my mind that Christians held to and loudly advocated for liberal, anti-biblical policies. Because of this, I took a significant amount of time to dig through the issues. In my research, one consistent theme I discovered was that Jesus would align more with liberal stances and policies because of His compassionate character, love, mild nature, etc. Genuinely trying to understand, I read the Gospels through "liberal glasses" (at least, to the best of my ability), attempting to see what they see.

I couldn't.

Despite every effort to do so, I could not see it; I didn't understand. And that bothered me. A lot.

So I kept wrestling—in prayer, Bible study, research, and conversations until I finally had a breakthrough. Well, two breakthroughs, actually. The first was that advocating anti-biblical policies (like abortion "rights") is just another expression of biblical illiteracy. People don't understand Scripture, so they align themselves (either ignorantly or intentionally) with stances that run contrary to it. On the surface, politics is a different category than the student examples described above, but it's the same underlying issue. This was my first and most fundamental realization, but I learned something else as well.

Before revealing the content of the second breakthrough, I want to note a caveat: I am painting in broad strokes. I'm not saying every Christian with liberal or apathetic tendencies falls into this category any more than I would claim every real Christian has a spotless church attendance record. But I can say with confidence that this *appears* to be true, inasmuch as my research and conversations have borne out.

So what was the breakthrough? What trend do I notice about Christians, particularly those with liberal tendencies?

Christians take Scripture, and particularly Jesus, out of context.

Instead of being responsible archeologists of Scripture—making every effort to present themselves to God as those who are approved, not needing to be ashamed, accurately handling the word of truth (2 Timothy 2:15), some focus too much on certain aspects of Jesus and either blatantly or subtly disregard others. Archeologists would be stripped of their titles and lose all their funding if they behaved this way. Keeping artifacts safely in their immediate context is imperative for their research and findings to have any validity.

Yet some Christians throw context out the window, picking apart the text and choosing to believe whatever serves their own purposes. Consequently, Jesus is often grossly transformed into a fluffy, mild, soft, cuddly character who lacks substance and cares more about a misconstrued distortion of love than He does truth. By taking Jesus out of context, they remove Him from the reality of God's Word. This makes Him a figment of our imagination, not revered in His true identity as the Son of God and Savior of the world.

In the next several chapters, we'll dig into some fallacies that have risen regarding Christ's identity—distinct yet detrimental ways some Christians take Jesus out of context and unfortunately inspire others to do the same. We will identify these myths and explore the truth (if any) within those arguments. Then, we'll discover where the truth gets distorted by lies due to faulty logic and erroneous hermeneutics practices. This step is crucial to flesh out, for then we can understand the origin of our mistakes in order to identify and avoid making them again in the future. Finally, we will discuss practical ramifications these myths have had on individuals, families, the church, and society at large. But before embarking on this journey, we need to do some housekeeping. We'll define the terms being used (please don't skip that chapter; it's crucial) and discuss the reasons these fallacies are such enormous issues within the church. I'm excited to go on this "dig" with you and allow the truth of God's Word to sharpen and mold us more into Christ's image.

Chapter Two

Defining Terms

Because these terms are familiar, the temptation will be to skip this chapter and move on to the "good stuff." I implore you to take the time to read through them, though. We often take terms and our understanding of them for granted. D. Martyn Lloyd Jones said, "We are living in an age when definitions are at a discount."[1] Far too often, we change them to suit what we like, asking what it means *to us*, instead of holding to objective definitions so we can have a productive conversation with others. Sometimes our understanding is accurate and thorough; other times, we are surprised by the ambiguity (or blatant error) with which we've been defining a term. Regardless, understanding these definitions is imperative for properly and accurately navigating the remainder of this book.

The Bible

The Bible is the inerrant, infallible, inspired, and living Word of God. The original autographs (first scrolls written by the original human authors of Bible) were 100 percent inerrant, meaning without error. Inerrancy refers to accuracy, factual integrity, and correctness. It encompasses every aspect of the Bible, from grammar to all aspects of theology. The copies we have today have been supernaturally preserved by God throughout many generations.[2] God is truth and is therefore factual, reliable, and precise, which is reflected in every word written in the Bible.

Whereas inerrancy refers to accuracy, infallibility refers to the *incapability of error*; namely, that the Bible is flawless and cannot be flawed because it reflects a flawless Author. The Bible can no more lead people astray (when interpreted correctly) than God could. This point is crucial, for within it (and others we'll explore), we recognize that God's Word is truth—absolute, unwavering, steadfast, foundational truth upon which our lives, both physical and eternal, are based. Because it reflects God and is a direct extension of Himself to us, Scripture is our authority. We do not impose ourselves or ideas on the Bible. Rather, we subject ourselves to it. The Bible, in its entirety, is truth for us to read, study, glean, meditate on, memorize, and hide in our hearts. It reveals truth; we are not at liberty to manipulate or remove pieces of it to suit our own purposes or agendas, much less define our "own" truth.

Scripture is also inspired—"All Scripture is inspired by God and profitable for teaching, for reproof, for correction, for training in righteousness" (2 Timothy 3:16). While we don't understand exactly how it happened, God inspired a few dozen men to write down the words He gave them. The words of Scripture may reflect the personality of their human authors, but not a single letter was written apart from God's explicit will.

Unlike every other book in the world, "the word of God is living and active and sharper than any two-edged sword, and piercing as far as the division of the soul and spirit, of both joints and marrow, and able to judge the thoughts and intentions of the heart" (Hebrews 4:12). In other words, it's alive. God is life, and He is the Author of life for all of creation and humanity. He uses His Word, first to introduce us to eternal life via the gospel, and then continually to breathe life into our souls through His Spirit working in and through Scripture to grow and mature us in our faith.

While it may seem obvious, we must realize that the Bible is, in fact, the Word of God. When Adam and Eve sinned in the Garden of Eden, their relationship with God was severely affected. They could no longer enjoy walking freely with Him as they had previously. Sin created a chasm between God and man. As a consequence, they suffered from broken communication with God. From then on, mankind needed an intercessor in order to communicate with Him. In the Old Testament, this happened through extensive ritual laws carried out by priests. Individuals understood the need to be clean and upright before praying to God (unless the subject of prayer was repentance, of course). Jesus later became the ultimate Mediator between God and man, and the Holy Spirit is our Helper today. But every system of communication after the fall—the Law, Jesus, and the Holy Spirit—uses the Word of God as the foundation for the communication. Instead of exclusively speaking to and through people verbally, God chose to write down and preserve His words so we would have access to them centuries later. What a gift!

The Bible has been God's primary method of communication with us since the fall. While He still speaks to individuals today, any genuine word received always supports or enhances His Word. It never contradicts it. The Holy Spirit illuminates the Bible so we can better understand it and thus be transformed into Christ's image. He never diminishes the Bible or points us away from it. Scripture is God's Word to us. It is perfect, holy, complete, and the only God-approved way to know and love Him while growing in sanctification.

Hermeneutics

Having a proper understanding of Scripture is crucial, but it accomplishes little if we don't know how to read, interpret, and apply it accurately to our lives. I will briefly explain hermeneutics here, but it will only scratch the surface of this deep and complex topic.

Hermeneutics is the method by which we read, interpret, and apply a text to our lives. Whether we realize it or not, we implement hermeneutical principles every time we read something—from instruction manuals and recipes to contracts and religious texts. *The most important aspect of hermeneutics is recognizing that we approach a text to discover what the author is saying; we do not impose our own meaning or ask, "What does it mean to me?"* If we're putting together a bookshelf and decide to switch the screws labeled "A" with the screws labeled "D" because we think they're prettier, the result will not be a sturdy bookshelf. However, when we read the manual and take the authors' instructions at their word, we'll be successful (assuming all parts are accounted for, of course).

The same is true, yet even more so, for the Bible. There is no text on earth we should take more seriously because, as we've discussed, it's the inerrant, infallible, inspired, and living Word of God. We should always approach it with holy reverence, giving it the respect due its Author. It is literally the book of life, not some self-help or fortune-telling book whose purpose is to tell us what we want to hear.

Readers approach Scripture in one of two ways—either by deductive or inductive reasoning and interpretation. Deduction means we start with a wide generalization or assumption and use it to determine specific details. Induction means we observe, collect, and organize details, and then we determine general principles from them. Consider a detective approaching a crime scene. If the detective began his investigation with a strong bias or an opinion about what happened, he would interpret the details of the crime scene to make them fit his theory. A responsible detective, however, implements inductive investigation methods by approaching the scene as a blank canvas. He gathers as many details and observations as possible. Then he organizes his discoveries and eventually draws a reasonable conclusion from them. See the difference? Deduction imposes one's predetermined thoughts onto details and makes them fit into his/her theory. Induction chooses to remain objective and to follow the evidence where it rightfully leads.

When we read Scripture, our only reasonable and responsible approach is induction. *The Bible does not exist to confirm our ideologies; it exists to determine them.*

How, then, are we to conduct inductive hermeneutics of Scripture? There are four rules of interpretation that, if heeded, will keep us on the straight and narrow path of accurate and responsible interpretation: 1) The literal, grammatical, historical method, 2) Scripture is the ultimate authority, 3) Context, and 4) Scripture interprets Scripture.

The Literal, Grammatical, and Historical Method

We approach inductive hermeneutics in one of three ways: textual criticism, the allegorical method, or the literal, grammatical, and historical method. You can probably guess which one is the most trustworthy approach, but we'll briefly review them for the sake of being thorough.

Textual critics aim to discover what the autographs of Scripture said. (Again, autographs were the original documents of Scripture, the ones all copies we have today were rendered from). While this is a noble goal, textual critics get so consumed with determining the exact characters of an ancient text, they neglect to move toward actual interpretation and application. That would be like a detective spending all his time gathering evidence from a crime scene but never doing anything with his findings. This kind of defeats the purpose. Thus, while some textual criticism is to be commended, we should never get so consumed with minute details and research that we neglect to move on to interpretation and application.

Whereas textual criticism bears some value, the allegorical method is deeply flawed. This method assumes Scripture is figurative and should rarely be applied literally. Advocates of this method also believe the reader determines when and how to apply the literal aspects. Again, deeply flawed. While the Bible does contain allegorical and figurative language (poetry, wisdom literature, and prophecies are full of it), there's a big difference between allegories within Scripture and allegorical Scripture. Promoters of the allegorical method believe that "fallible, fallen, sinful, and debilitated people have the right to determine when the infallible, perfect, holy, and true God is being literal or not, when He Himself makes no such distinction. It's at once laughable and utterly disheartening."[3]

The third inductive hermeneutics option is by far the best and most responsible: the literal, grammatical, and historical method. Put simply, this method upholds three fundamental rules of interpretation. First, Scripture is written literally and should be interpreted as such unless the language or context surrounding it demands otherwise. Second, we should always apply traditional, well-accepted rules of grammar when reading it. Again, when reading an instruction manual, we don't switch the screws around because we think that's what the author was "really" trying to say. Instead, we take it at face value and interpret it appropriately. Lastly, Scripture was written at specific times, in specific places, by specific people, for specific purposes. In other words, every part of Scripture has a historical context, and proper hermeneutics demands that we never separate context from the text itself.

Scripture Is the Ultimate Authority

Because Scripture is the inerrant, infallible, inspired, and living Word of God, it is our authority. We never impose our own "authority" onto it. One question you've probably heard numerous times in various studies is, "What does this verse (or passage) mean to you?" While that may sound insightful and a good way to prompt discussion, this question is dangerous. It assumes the reader and his/her opinion are more important than the passage itself. As harsh as this may sound, who cares what we think? Why would anyone waste time exploring the thoughts of mere man when we could explore the thoughts of the One who created him? We should instead ask, "What does this passage mean?" and then, "How can we apply its truth (or theological principle) to our lives?"

Our job as readers is not to impose, change, "clarify," or manipulate the truths of Scripture to accommodate our opinions and preferences. We all approach Scripture with certain biases and perspectives (we all have baggage). But our goal should be to identify our baggage, put it aside, and come to Scripture with dedicated intent to discover truth as God reveals it, not as how we think it would be most beneficial to us. While Jesus is our Friend, He is first our King. We stand in complete subjection to Him as His followers. We are not His peers. We are humble servants attempting to gather every morsel of truth from His table and apply it to our lives so we can be more transformed into His image.

One final note on this: proper interpretation, application, and life transformation through Scripture happens only in partnership with the Holy Spirit. The Bible is God's Word, and only He can release His life-giving power through its pages. Partnering with the Holy Spirit ultimately means acknowledging and depending on Him while we study Scripture. We should never approach the Bible as some kind of independent auditor, hoping to glean some interesting information. Rather, we pray—humbly asking God, through His Spirit, who indwells our hearts—that we can responsibly understand and apply the words He so graciously gives. That's a prayer He is always happy to answer.

Context, Context, Context!

You may have realized that I'm a fan of this word. It is, in fact, the entire purpose of this book. It really is *that* important. Before starting to work toward my master's degree, I joined a short-term missions team in Cambodia for two weeks. While there, we encountered some…interesting cultural peculiarities. One of our young men had befriended a Khmer student, obviously with the hope of sharing the gospel with him. A couple of days into their friendship, the student reached for our young man's hand, wanting to hold it as they walked along the street. Since holding hands is a gesture of romance in our American culture, our team member grew quite uncomfortable. Much to his credit, however, he took it in stride, realizing that in Cambodia, holding hands (even between men), is a sign of friendship. If our teammate had responded as he normally would have in America, he would have greatly offended his new Khmer friend. But with great wisdom, he understood the context of his immediate situation and bolstered a friendship because of it.

Context matters. Whether in a foreign country or reading the Bible, we must pay attention to context if we're to have success in our endeavors.

In the Bible, some verses are easy to interpret and apply apart from studied context, like "Be kind to one another," found in Ephesians 4:32. We don't need an advanced degree or even much intellect to deduce the applicable meaning of that statement. However, many (if not most) Scripture passages require a bit more work if we're to understand them fully, within their original context. (And even Ephesians 4:32 goes from black and white to full color when we realize the context in which it was written.) Again, every sentence of Scripture was written at a particular time, in a particular place, by a particular person inspired by God, to a particular people, for a particular purpose. Reading and interpreting truths of Scripture without knowing these most basic facts will render proper interpretation and application exceedingly difficult, if not impossible.

Would you ever pick up an unfamiliar novel, flip to a random middle page, read a sentence or two, and then claim to know what's going on and what it's about? Hardly. Yet we do this with Scripture all the time. We simply cannot be good stewards of God's Word without diligently putting every passage we read into context.

While this may sound overwhelming, especially if it's new to you, take heart. The more you learn, the more you know; the more you know, the more you'll grow. You may have to go back and brush up on contexts of previous passages you've studied, but for the most part, once you've completed a thorough study of a book of Scripture, you'll remember enough at least to get you started on the right track in future studies. It's like riding a bike—the more you do it, the easier it becomes.

Scripture Interprets Scripture

Lastly, when reading the Bible, we must recognize that Scripture interprets Scripture. This may sound funny, but part of understanding context is knowing that we must read the Bible in light of itself. Scripture is one book comprised of sixty-six smaller, individual volumes. Some are letters, some are historical narratives, some are poetry, etc. But while they are unique, they are not completely independent of each other, for they all have the same ultimate Author: God. Thus, when we glean theological truths from one passage, we should always compare them with the same truths presented elsewhere in Scripture—first to confirm, and then to provide us with a fuller, more elaborate picture of the truth we're studying.

This is especially important when reading two texts that seem to contradict each other. When we dig deeper, understanding the context of each passage individually before determining the theological principles present in each, we eventually realize they don't contradict. They are simply two ways—two perspectives—of communicating the same truth. Why is that important? One huge reason is because it helps us know God more. By reading Scripture in light of itself and wrestling with seeming discrepancies, we realize just how magnificent, complex, and multi-dimensional God is. He could have easily given us a monotonous dish with Scripture. Instead, He gave us a complex, nutrient-dense feast that entices all our senses and causes us to appreciate Him and His truth that much more.

In conclusion, we all practice hermeneutics. The question is whether we practice it responsibly and in a way that glorifies God, or whether we impose our own thoughts, ideas, and biases on Scripture, twisting it to conform to our agendas. As Christians, our only option is the first. If we claim to know, love, and want to honor God, we must accept His Word as our ultimate authority, submit to its truth, and conduct due diligence while reading, interpreting, and applying it to our lives.

Truth

Truth is the absolute, unwavering reality of established facts anchored in and revealed by the God of the Bible. Two methods of revelation exist to communicate truth to humanity—special revelation and general revelation. Special revelation is truth revealed in Scripture, primarily revealing the spiritual reality of the gospel and eternal life available and awaiting us with God through Christ. Jesus is the ultimate form of special revelation, "for in Him all the fullness of Deity dwells in bodily form" (Colossians 2:9). General revelation, however, is what God has communicated through the physical world and universe. We glean these facts through scientific research and experience—verified accuracies that may not reveal God directly but do reveal truths about Him (i.e., His sovereignty, omnipotence, omniscience, creativity, etc.)

General revelation subjects itself to special revelation. This means special revelation informs general revelation, not the other way around. Science is wonderful, methodical, and one of the surest ways to draw conclusions about the way the world works. But scientists have been wrong numerous times and on numerous issues, only to be corrected years later. Even the terminology scientists use reveals their hesitancy to make an absolute claim. "Hypotheses" are educated guesses that attempt to answer scientific questions. Yet, they must be tested over and over, in different ways, using different methods. If scientists find promising and consistent results, the answer is then deemed a scientific theory. *Theory*, not fact. Even scientific laws (observable realities like the laws of gravity and motion) remain mysterious to scientists in both how and why they work the way they do. Scientists attempt to form the best theories to explain them, but in the end, no human can ever have a complete, unwavering, and comprehensive grasp of any aspect of science.

Why? Because the created can never fully understand the Creator. Science can neither prove nor disprove God, despite many efforts on both sides to do so. But an astute observer can use science to learn more about God and how He created the world, which should be the ultimate goal of general revelation:

> For the wrath of God is revealed from heaven against all ungodliness and unrighteousness of men who suppress the truth in unrighteousness, because that which is known about God is evident within them; for God made it evident to them. For since the creation of the world His invisible attributes, His eternal power and divine nature, have been clearly seen, being understood through what has been made, so that they are without excuse. (Romans 1:18–20)

Do tensions exist between science and God? Do some scientific findings seem to contradict Scripture? Yes. But many more reveal and confirm the truth of God as revealed in His Word. In the end, ascribing to either science or God requires faith. Science constantly changes, so putting your trust in it requires faith to accept the ever-shifting sand of general revelation found in scientific discoveries and theories. This will, as it has in the past, require admitting the "facts" you're so sure of now can potentially be proven wrong later, as more information is discovered. The alternative is to put your faith in God, the Author of all information, scientific and otherwise. Putting your faith in God means trusting the Creator and Sustainer of all things. It means acknowledging (and resting in) the fact that sure and steady truth exists and that you don't have to understand it all, because the One who is sovereign over everything does.

Because all truth (special and general) is anchored in God, it cannot and never will be subjective, changing, or open to manipulation. God does not change. We have the blessed hope of realizing that even when something doesn't make sense to us, we can trust the One who makes sense of everything in the end. Further, our lack of understanding on certain matters should reassure us. Would you entrust your current worldview and eternal destiny to someone who is only your peer? I certainly wouldn't! Only a God far beyond our comprehension is worthy of our faith, trust, and admiration. Truth is absolute, unwavering, and anchored in the Author, Creator, and Sustainer of the universe as revealed through creation and the special revelation of the Bible.

Christian

The term "Christian" was originally used in Antioch in the first century. It literally means "little Christ." A Christian is someone who has come to faith in Christ through the gospel and has given his or her life to follow Him as a disciple. The gospel (or good news) can be defined as:

> The good news of God's plan to rescue a spiritually dead, broken, condemned, and sin-enslaved world, offering forgiveness of sin, eternal life, and the restoration of peace with Him through the comprehensive and final sacrifice of Jesus Christ— who was born of a virgin, lived a sinless life, died on the cross, was buried, and rose again—bringing us to life in Him, adopting us into His family, and securing us in His glorious future.

Christians believe, ascribe to, and base their current lives and eternal destinies on the gospel and the truth of God's Word (as previously defined). Being a Christian is not merely adding a title to our identities. It's the transformation of our identity from death to life, from lost to found, from broken to whole.

A Christian is not someone who says a rote prayer once, then goes about his merry way, thinking his entrance into heaven one day is secured. Rather, to become a Christian is to enter into a relationship with God Almighty and begin to be transformed into His image through the predestined plan of the Father, the power of Christ and His resurrection, and the sanctifying work of the Holy Spirit in our lives.

While we receive the gospel through faith alone, evidence of our faith is revealed in the way we live our lives thereafter. Christians are far from perfect, but we consistently strive to grow in our sanctification. We actively pursue both knowledge of and increased love for God through prayer, Bible study, fellowship with other believers, frequent repentance of sin, and obedience to God's Word. Just as healthy, living trees produce fruit, so genuine, thriving Christians will produce the fruit of the Holy Spirit in their lives.

Many subsects of Christianity exist, seen predominantly in the myriad of church denominations that are around today. Many differ only in worship preference and slight differences of opinion regarding secondary theological interpretations (i.e., the Lord's Supper, baptism, end times, etc.). However, some that have risen over recent decades take much greater liberties when interpreting Scripture. In this volume, we will refer to these denominations (and members therein) as liberal and traditional denominations as conservative.

Liberal

Defining Terms

We can define a liberal person many ways, but the definition for our discussion will remain philosophical and essential, not strictly political: a liberal is someone who is open to new thoughts, experiences, and theories to the point of compromising (or even disavowing) truth. Psychologist Jonathan Haidt, a self-proclaimed liberal, describes liberals as those wanting a society of people that is open, changing, and ever evolving.[4]

His definition sounds lovely, and it's certainly appealing. After all, isn't open-mindedness a good thing? Who wants to be closed-minded and reject new experiences? Who wants to be accused of being bull-headed and against change?

Unfortunately, it's not quite as easy or as simple as it seems.

Before investigating the not-so-great aspects of liberal philosophies, we must acknowledge the good. Open-mindedness, to some extent, is most certainly a good thing. A child who eats only French fries and refuses all other cuisine will stunt his nutrition and development, making him weak and prone to all kinds of health deficiencies. Or, for a more substantial example, consider Louis Braille. At age fifteen, he was not content with the clumsy, awkward, impractical system of reading that existed for the blind, so he decided to do something about it. It took years, but he eventually developed a new system, which is now the universal standard: Braille. If Louis hadn't been open-minded, if he hadn't challenged the system, determined to make things better in spite of strong opposition, the world wouldn't have the easy, convenient system of Braille today.

Open-mindedness is beneficial in numerous ways, for it recognizes that we each come from unique positions, colored by our personalities, backgrounds, experiences, talents, and passions. Our opinions are no more valid than someone else's simply because they're ours. We are not superior to others in value or worth. It also encourages us to think outside the box—to push, stretch, and be creative in finding solutions to problems we face in the world.

If our existence was limited to the temporal and physical, then liberal philosophies would be both admirable and a solid standard for society to pursue. Again, open-mindedness and acceptance of change have many benefits. However, our existence is far more than physical, and this is where many liberal philosophies go awry. We are first spiritual beings, created in God's image for the purpose of glorifying Him. To limit our existence or prioritize our agendas to only the physical world is to severely handicap or even void any eternal purpose we have on earth. And therein lies a glaring flaw of liberal ideologies—it leaves little to no room for the spiritual realm, which is the greater and truer reality than what we experience with our senses on earth.

"But wait!" you exclaim. "I have friends who are liberals and are also very spiritual. They follow Buddha and even dapple in Hindu thought. And they appreciate all spirituality and the majority of religions." Ah, but therein lies another fallacy. Every religion claims to be true—*the* authentic path to God, a higher power, or the ultimate version of one's true self. Religions fiercely contradict each other. By that fact alone, we acknowledge the most fundamental, essential point of this entire argument—*truth exists, and it is absolute. It is not subjective or relative to one's personal experience.* Why? Because it exists outside ourselves and outside the physical realm.

It's wonderful—even commendable—to exercise our creativity and open-mindedness in order to pursue or further understand truth. But when truth is compromised in the name of open-mindedness, we have crossed an inexcusable line. This is where most self-professing liberals find themselves. They boast of their open-mindedness, specifically as it relates to the destruction, deconstruction, and/or "clarification" of truth. Truth, in their minds, is an archaic construct of generations past to keep people in line. They claim that people need to be liberated from it in order to be free. Many liberals reject the existence of absolute truth, and they exercise all kinds of creative measures to get around arguments for it. Even some churches have taken this stance. One "church" in Atlanta, Georgia, went on record saying the Bible is not the Word of God, and while it does contain good principles, it is not the source of truth.

Yikes.

Anyone who blatantly rejects the authority, inspiration, and infallibility of the Bible is by definition *not* a Christian. You simply cannot claim to be a Christ-follower or disciple of Christ and not believe what He did and said, especially something as foundational as the validity and truth of Scripture. Jesus is the Word incarnate; the Truth personified. It is both an insult and grave offense to bear His name and ignore His very identity.

Yet some go further and declare that truth doesn't exist. Unfortunately, they fail to realize that "there is no absolute truth" is a self-defeating statement. The speaker declared a presumed fact in an imperative statement, claiming it is absolutely true that no absolute truth exists. This, of course, is nonsense. Any attentive listeners should immediately discredit the speaker.

Thus, while liberal ideologies of open-mindedness can be good, useful, and beneficial in some instances, there is a hard and fast line that cannot be crossed. That line? Truth. When we disregard truth, our "open-mindedness" quickly transforms into delusion—thoughts or desires that can never and will never be grounded in reality, either physical or spiritual.

As with every worldview, there is a spectrum amidst liberal philosophies. Some liberals reject any and all forms of objective truth, which makes faith in God impossible. Yet some Christians consider themselves liberals. While impossible to describe every possible philosophical makeup of those ascribing to this title, they all must adhere to one common absolute in order to retain authenticity within the label:

> *Any Christian, liberal or conservative, is first a Christian, and therefore must by definition believe in the absolute truth of Scripture. He/she must also do everything within their power to embrace God's transformation in his/her life through the gospel of Jesus Christ as worked out by the power of the Holy Spirit.*

Disagreements exist within nuances of theology, politics, and historical, grammatical, and literal hermeneutical conclusions of the Bible. However, we must hold Scripture as the authority over everyone who bears the title Christian. One simply cannot be a Christian, as defined and exemplified by Jesus, otherwise.

Conservative

A conservative can be defined as someone who is cautious with change, who holds firmly to and "conserves" traditional values. While the definition of a liberal sounds immediately appealing, this definition makes it sound as if conservatives are bunch of Neanderthals, choosing to bury their heads in the sand instead of embracing life. Admittedly, we could accurately describe some conservatives as such—completely shut down in their perspective and unwilling even to entertain the notion of change. However, many conservatives are not that way at all. Rather, they *choose* to uphold traditional values after having thoughtfully considered the alternatives.

While variations exist, conservatives (theologically speaking) define "traditional values" biblically when they abide by the previously defined rules of hermeneutics. Thus, conservatives believe in and are dedicated to upholding solid, unwavering foundations in their beliefs, actions, and faith. In order to understand what conservatives believe, it may be helpful to acknowledge where conservativism *can* go wrong. However, we must immediately recognize a significant caveat— conservatives, like liberals, cannot be universally defined by their few extreme members.

First, some conservatives, but certainly not all, believe change is bad. Conservatives have made many critical discoveries and accomplished much in medicine, psychology, science, the arts, business, and more. These conservatives never would have pursued these changes if they were content with the way things were. (Louis Braille was a devout Catholic.)

Conservatives appreciate and pursue positive change—but not change regarding their fundamental values and beliefs.

Second, outlying conservatives may think poorly of people who hold different values, but this is not true with the majority, and certainly not those holding to biblical values. Obviously, there's plenty of hate and judgment on both sides of worldview philosophies, but the majority of conservatives are regular people who contribute positively to society. They do not hate or harbor ill will toward others who do not agree with them. In fact, the opposite is true. Christian conservatives are called to love others, even and especially those who don't align with their every perspective.

Third, conservatives can be stubborn for the sake of being stubborn, but blind stubbornness is not the pulse of the majority. While conservatives hold fast to certain values, it's because they have explored and considered other options and decided traditional values bear truth and wisdom to live by.

Perhaps an analogy would be beneficial. Think of liberals and conservatives each sailing their own vessel on the open sea. Liberals may begin with a destination—or not. If they do, they're open to changing their destination if circumstances or the weather changes. They prioritize enjoying the journey above than the final destination. Christian liberals have both a destination (to glorify God and enjoy Him forever) and the map (the Bible), but they leave lots of room for stops and scenic routes along the way.

Conservatives use a more focused approach. They have the destination (to glorify God and enjoy Him forever), as well as the map (the Bible). The difference with conservatives is that those two foundations guide and direct every decision they make along their journey. They do not waver from the map (at least, not intentionally and/or without repentance), and they're committed to following the map as precisely as they can. Their perspective aligns with George Whitefield, who said, "If we once get above our Bibles and cease making them the written Word of God our sole rule both as to faith and practice, we shall soon lie open to all manner of delusion and be in great danger of making shipwreck of faith and a good conscience."[5]

While conservatives "live by the Book," there's still ample room for us to decide how to follow the map. Again, they utilize creativity in pursuing truth to glorify God, but they don't disregard truth for a "higher" or "more inspired" interpretation. Some people advocate following both the ship's manufacturing instructions and the map. Others rely on life experience and collective wisdom and go from there. But overall, conservatives try to live focused lives, allowing Scripture and their ultimate end of glorifying God and enjoying Him forever to impact every decision they make along the way. They follow the advice, "Press forward. Do not stop, do not linger in your journey, but strive for the mark set before you."[6]

Fourth, one tendency toward error in conservative circles is that they abide by truth for the sake of tradition, not transformation. They may read, interpret, and even apply Scripture properly, but it remains head knowledge and never manifests itself in their hearts. Thus, like Pharisees in the New

Testament, their lives look devout, righteous, and pure on the outside. They can quote Scripture forward and backward, teach Sunday school, and lead someone to Christ. But they simply go through the motions. They are the "elder brothers" of Luke 15—people who live by the rules because they believe this will get them what they want. They don't love God, nor do they have a transformative, thriving relationship with Him through Christ. They merely use His name and ways of living to propagate their own interests. They live for the accolades of men instead of the glory of God.

We must avoid this as much as possible. To combat religiosity and embrace humility, we must constantly ask ourselves "Why?" Why do we read the Bible? Why do we memorize it? Why do we vote a particular way? Why do we raise our children as we do? What shapes our work ethic? The goal of this exercise is to determine our motivation. If our motivation is to bring God glory, the grace of God through Jesus Christ has successfully bridged the chasm between our minds and hearts. If not, we need to reevaluate, repent, and beg God to engage our hearts as we pursue His truth.

A final misnomer about conservatives is that, while some are admittedly unreasonable, that is the exception, not the norm. Conservatives can (and often do) discuss and debate people of other worldviews rationally and in the context of love. But here's the insurmountable roadblock that's so often misunderstood (or not acknowledged at all): a conservative's worldview is literally incompatible with a liberal's because the foundation of our belief is Scripture, and (most) liberals do not share that tenet. If truth is not a presumed fact, and if it's not defined by God according to Scripture, debating will ultimately be a fruitless exercise between liberals and conservatives.

The Problem in the Church

Some liberals profess to be Christians and to base their beliefs in Scripture. The problem is that many either deliberately or unknowingly reject the truth of Scripture. This happens largely because they don't know how to read, interpret, and apply Scripture in ways that honor God and maintain the integrity of His gospel. The consequences of such misunderstanding are dire. In generations past, the broadly accepted pulse within evangelical communities was the conservative application of truth. But now we see liberal applications as church members engage in behavior that directly contradicts the Bible, yet they rationalize and justify this behavior by saying, "Well, this is what Jesus would do." For example, some approve (in conscience and actions) gay marriage, which blatantly defies God's created mandate. They make many excuses and twist the Bible like a pretzel to justify such views. But therein lies the point: while their mission may be genuinely heartfelt, neither naïveté nor direct disobedience is ever excusable for the Christian. In fact, misunderstanding, misinterpreting, and disobeying Scripture for any reason (much less to appeal to or make peace with worldly philosophies) is sin. It doesn't advance the gospel; it impedes it. What's worse, it invites others down a path of deceit and confusion that can irreparably harm their very souls. Such pollution of truth accomplishes Satan's agenda of leading people away from God and His gospel. These advocates genuinely believe heaven stands by their beliefs and actions, when in reality, the demons of hell rejoice over their stances.

As stated above, every Christian, liberal or conservative, is a Christian first and foremost. Being a Christian means bearing the name and identity of Christ in our thoughts, speech, actions, and interactions with the world around us. Thus, our primary pursuit should be to believe and live out the truths of God's Word as read and interpreted in its proper context. Only then are we faithful and diligent stewards of absolute truth.

That's why this book exists—to explain biblical truths on specific topics, thereby debunking erroneous claims that attempt to use Jesus to promote liberal, wayward agendas. Everyone who bears Jesus's name must learn to keep Him in His rightful, honoring Biblical context. For Christians, our identity is found in the truth of God's Word, which is uncompromisable and not open to whimsical interpretation.

Chapter Three
Complicating the Issue

As we discussed in the previous two chapters, a major issue in our current culture and churches is that Christians (and non-Christians) take Jesus out of context, removing Him from the sacred Word of God. This is hardly a new problem; people have been doing this for centuries. Some intentionally and deliberately seek their own agenda and willfully lead others astray. Most, however, do so ignorantly, not understanding they're believing falsehoods about Jesus. Though many factors contribute to this error, the one we will target in this book is this: *every plausible lie contains at least a small measure of truth.*

Satan is the master of deception and the primary agent behind the movement of taking Jesus out of context. The devil dangles a healthy dose of truth into his webs of lies, which makes him an exceedingly powerful force. He knows that Jesus-followers would easily recognize obvious, outright lies and reject them. So, he includes just enough truth to make Christians pause, question their previous understanding of God's Word, and then believe the lies the nugget of truth is immersed in.

Two examples will shed light on his methods of deception: Adam and Eve in the Garden of Eden and Jesus in the wilderness. We'll explore both to discover how Satan skillfully wraps his deception in strips of truth. We'll also learn how to avoid his snares in our own journeys—both conceptually and practically through study of specific theological tenet.

Adam and Eve

When God placed Adam and Eve in the garden, He gave them only one restriction: "From any tree of the garden you may eat freely, but from the tree of the knowledge of good and evil you shall not eat, for in the day that you eat from it you will surely die" (Genesis 2:16–17). Adam and Eve could literally do anything they wanted except eat from one single tree. God certainly didn't make it complicated. So how would Satan get them to disobey? How would he convince two people completely unfamiliar with sin to choose death over life?

He would manipulate God's Word to serve his evil purposes.

First, he identified his victim and prepared the environment. He targeted Eve, which directly usurped the hierarchy of headship God established in creation; namely, that Adam was to lead, protect, and provide for his wife. Next, he waited until Eve (with Adam nearby) was close to the tree of knowledge of good and evil. The saying, "out of sight, out of mind," is highly accurate. Satan knew his chances of success would increase if Eve was within eyeshot of the tree. If she had to walk to the tree from far away, she would have had ample time to reevaluate and change her mind.

Next, Satan asked a question. "Indeed, has God said, 'You shall not eat from any tree of the garden'?" This tactic is crucial and must not be overlooked. By asking Eve a question, he both disarms Eve and invites her to ask questions as well. Questions are inviting; imperatives are sinister. Satan could have begun by directly contradicting the Lord: "God didn't say that!" But Eve would have shut down that conversation then and there. Satan's claim would have had no validity, and Eve would have had no reason to entertain him further. But that's not what happened. Satan chose to ask a question—to appear as an ally rather than a foe and to enter the conversation in the least-threatening way possible.

In addition to starting the conversation on a casual note and questioning God, Satan invites Eve to question God herself. Adam and Eve had probably never even thought about questioning God's mandate. They loved Him and obeyed Him out of that love. But by asking questions about it and then subtly contradicting it, Satan opened the door for Eve to question and begin weighing the pros and cons of her obedience. In other words, he attempted to open her mind to new possibilities that may exist outside God and His Word.

As a quick aside, the possibility of "secret knowledge" or discovering some new way to live is still a huge lure for people today. We like making discoveries. We love unearthing something new that we can share with others and gain bragging rights for the discovery. Trends exist for a reason. People are quick to jump on the bandwagon of new fashions, ideologies, gadgets, hobbies, politics, décor, spiritual pursuits, etc. New is often synonymous with exciting. It invites us to break out of our routine and breathe fresh inspiration into our souls. Yet as with any aspect of our lives, wisdom calls for us to examine new thoughts, ideas, and trends by first subjecting them to the truth of Scripture. We could avoid much harm if we took the time to destroy "speculations and every lofty thing raised up against the knowledge of God," and take "every thought captive to the obedience of Christ."[7] Eve would've avoided catastrophic consequences if she had done so.

Eve's reply to Satan's initial question is revealing:

> "From the fruit of the trees of the garden we may eat;
> but from the fruit of the tree which is in the middle
> of the garden, God has said, 'You shall not eat from
> it or touch it, or you will die.'"

Even though posed as a question, Satan's query seemed to invoke a sense of defensiveness in Eve, for she added an unnecessary detail. It is almost as if she threw up extra barricades to protect herself from the crafty serpent. God never told Adam (at least in recorded word) that they could not *touch* the tree. He said only that they could not *eat* of it. Thus, either Adam and Eve collectively agreed to establish an extra layer of protection around themselves by refusing even to touch it, or Eve got flustered by Satan's question and erected additional fortifications of her own.

The next tactic Satan used was perceived flippant defiance: "You surely will not die!" It's as if he threw back his head and laughed at the silliness of Eve's ignorance. This is crucial because in this statement *he made light of God's Word*. He invited her to see it, not as the unwavering foundation upon which she must live, move, hope, and base every decision, but as something to question, something *that was open to change*. And lest we miss the most obvious part of this statement, it's a blatant lie. Satan consistently weaves just enough truth in his lies to keep them plausible so he can invite us to dwell on them. But not here. He directly contradicted what God told Adam in Genesis 2:17. Wrapping it in a flippant tone lessened the impact, but make no mistake: this is a blunt affront to God's word and character.

Continuing, he said, "'For God knows that in the day you eat from it your eyes will be opened and you will be like God, knowing good and evil.'" Amidst his flippant treatment of God's Word, Satan employed another tactic, "clarifying" what God meant when He gave His directive. Oh, the sneaky brilliance of this fallen creature! If we didn't hate him so much, we'd be tempted to admire him.

By attempting to clarify what God meant, Satan placed himself—*his interpretation*—above what God actually said. Once that happens, God's Word can be changed to suit whatever the "interpreter" desires, which inevitably strips God's Word of its power and renders it void. Satan did exactly that with his "clarification." He told Eve that God may have said that, but it's not what He *meant*. And with this, Satan proposed a "new truth," a fresh, deeper, more profound way of understanding God. He suggested that *he* held the real truth about God and His motivations, over and beyond what God Himself has spoken.

Satan deceived Eve into believing he cared for her more than God did. Indeed, Satan claimed to be the one opening her eyes and showing her the "real truth." This suggests that her eyes, until this point, had been closed; that she had not been privy to "inside information." She'd been ignorant about something that could change her life forever, and God was the One who wanted to keep her in the dark.

The infuriating part of Satan's shrewd and brutal affront is that it contains some truth. Adam and Eve had been living without certain knowledge; facts existed that they did not know about. God told them they would die, but He didn't reveal every consequence and ramification that would occur if they ate the fruit. But contrary to what Satan led them to believe, he didn't care about their enlightenment. He cared only about their destruction. Eating the forbidden fruit would have opened their eyes and made them like God in the sense that they would have knowledge of both good and evil they hadn't known before. But that knowledge would be anything but beneficial. In reality, that knowledge would cause immediate and irreversible oppression by their sin and, ultimately, death. Satan, of course, conveniently left out that part. Instead, he wrapped the nugget of truth (being like God) in a manipulative lie designed to lure Eve to sure death.

And it worked.

Instead of rebuking Satan and his dismissively erroneous understanding of God's Word, Eve pondered it. She allowed the seed of doubt to take root in her once-pure soil of faith. She turned her eyes from the Lord and the truth to Satan and his deceptive postulations:

> When the woman saw that the tree was good for food,
> and that it was a delight to the eyes, and that the tree
> was desirable to make one wise… (Genesis 3:6a)

I imagine that, for a moment, the universe held its breath, wanting to rage against Eve's temptation. But all remained silent. The lions didn't roar, the wind didn't thrust itself at Eve to divert her from the Tempter. The trees didn't shake their leaves, nor did the rocks cry out. Angels didn't come down with swords and do away with Satan once and for all. No force of nature, no member of the animal kingdom, no angelic realm uttered a word of warning or intervention. God kept the earth silent and remained silent Himself.

Why?

Why didn't everyone and everything throw themselves at Eve to remind her of the truth? Why didn't someone shock her out of her momentary bout of delusion and draw her back into the safety of the divine reality God created in Eden?

Because she had to choose for herself.

Both she and Adam had been told the truth, maybe not every detail of what "death" consisted of, but certainly enough to trust and obey. God wasn't sneaky, nor was He cruel. He didn't say, "There is one tree you can't eat from," and then refuse to identify it. He didn't make them figure it out on their own by trial and error. He told them the truth and gave them the choice to follow it. In turn, they understood and had chosen to believe it. They rested in the security of their choice, experiencing the bliss of perfection, harmony, peace, and joy. They were fully informed of God's will, and were without excuse for not complying.

And as with most choices we make, Adam and Eve had to continue making it. If we choose to eat healthier, that decision has to last longer than one meal. It needs to be a continual choice we make daily if we want it to have any positive benefit. Likewise, Adam and Eve had to continue making the choice not to eat the fruit of the tree of the knowledge of good and evil. Every time they felt a little pang of hunger, they had to decide to avoid that fruit. In order to obey God, they continually had to choose to do so. It may have become a habit—something easy to obey because of the pattern they had developed. But it was still a choice, and one they continued making day in and day out. Thus, when Satan presented an alternative choice to Eve, it wasn't as if she went from having no choice to having the ability to choose. Rather, she went from choosing to abide by truth to choosing to succumb to a lie.

Let's explore the sequence of events immediately leading up to her detrimental choice. First, she "saw that the tree was good for food," which brings us back to the "out of sight, out of mind" reference from earlier. The tree was most definitely *in sight* for Eve (part of Satan's initial strategy). This seems to indicate this was the first time she took time to look at it. Knowing and believing that tree was against God's will would likely have prevented Eve from ever looking closely at it. After all, why pay attention to something you've already decided isn't worth it?

But now things have changed. Instead of looking to and for God, she looked to the thing that will sever her relationship with Him. For probably the first time, something other than God looked good to Eve. And therein lies another point to consider: Satan is never going to tempt you with anything that looks unappealing. Temptations vary significantly, and what may tempt me might never tempt you. One of my mentors in college used to tell me that Satan would never tempt me with extramarital sex, drugs, and alcohol because he knew those held no appeal for me. Rather, he would tempt me with saying yes to too many things—he would tempt me with busy-ness (even good activities) that would render me useless for what I was supposed to do. (This has happened more times than I'd like to admit.) The point is that temptations always look good; they are always "a delight to the eyes." God didn't make that fruit puke-green, moldy, lumpy, and reeking with foul odors. It wouldn't surprise me if it was the most beautiful, attractive fruit in the whole garden. If temptations weren't *tempting*, they wouldn't require much of a *choice*—our faith would not be tried and subsequently strengthened if we held fast.

The fruit looked "good for food" and was "a delight to the eyes," but it was also "desirable to make one wise." With that phrase, we move from the superficial, physical aspect of the temptation to the metaphysical and spiritual. The fruit did not merely tempt her physical senses (sight and appetite). It also tempted her pride. She wanted to be wise…like God. She was no longer content being a humble child who trusted her Father. She wanted to be like Him—to be wise like Him.

Many a Christian has fallen into sin and heresy for this very reason. The unfortunate part is that there's nothing wrong with wanting to be wise. In fact, God encourages us to pursue wisdom:

> A wise man will hear and increase in learning, and a
> man of understanding will acquire wise counsel…
> The fear of the LORD is the beginning of
> knowledge; fools despise wisdom and instruction.
> (Proverbs 1:5,7)

The secret of this pursuit, however, lies in the origin of wisdom—the Lord. "For the LORD gives wisdom; from His mouth come knowledge and understanding" (Proverbs 2:6). Where we err, like Eve, is in looking *outside* God and His Word for wisdom. We erroneously and naively think we can become more like God by seeking wisdom apart from Him. This, of course, is ridiculous, because no wisdom (or truth) can be found apart from God or outside what He has revealed. It's like wanting to learn more about your car and deciding your baker knows more about transmissions than your mechanic does. This is absolutely nonsensical, yet we do it all the time in various ways. We seek wisdom on social media, news, self-help books, friends…pretty much anything except its Source, Creator, and Sustainer.

The truth is that we can never become more like God (which should be every Christian's goal) except by immersing ourselves in His Word and abiding by it:

> "Abide in Me, and I in you. As the branch cannot
> bear fruit of itself unless it abides in the vine, so
> neither can you unless you abide in Me. I am the
> vine, you are the branches; he who abides in Me and
> I in him, he bears much fruit, for apart from Me you
> can do nothing." (John 15:4–5)

Eve wanted to be more like God, but her method of choice would lead her in the exact opposite direction. Instead of abiding in God's word, she relied on a secret she thought she'd found—a new way of doing things, a clever path that would bypass God's mandates yet accomplish the same goal. The result was her demise, and the demise of all created beings.

How often do we do the same? Psychology, culture, philosophy, education, and even religions have been trying for centuries to establish wisdom apart from God. They think believing in God and Jesus is foolish, elementary, and reserved for those incapable of deep thought on their own. They view religion as a crutch and believe themselves above it because they pursue wisdom through other venues. Our "woke" culture today displays exactly that, except instead of moving toward wisdom, it moves humanity deeper into self-absorbed delusion. "Waking up" is actually falling deeper into spiritual slumber. And it's been happening for centuries:

> For the word of the cross is foolishness to those who are perishing, but to us who are being saved it is the power of God. For it is written, "I will destroy the wisdom of the wise, and the cleverness of the clever I will set aside." Where is the wise man? Where is the scribe? Where is the debater of this age? Has not God made foolish the wisdom of the world? For since in the wisdom of God the world through its wisdom did not come to know God…the foolishness of God is wiser than men, and the weakness of God is stronger than men. (1 Corinthians 1:18–21a, 25)

Wisdom without God is but a myth, a mirage. Eve was the first person to believe she could attain wisdom apart from Him, but she's certainly not been the last. The consequences of our unbelief today stem from hers several millennia ago.

After seeing how desirable the fruit was, both physically and spiritually, "she took from its fruit and ate; and she gave also to her husband with her, and he ate" (Genesis 3:6b). Two points are worth noting here. First, being tempted is not a sin in itself. The next passage we will discuss is about Jesus's temptation in the wilderness. As with Eve, Satan directly tempted Jesus. Unlike Eve, He did not sin. Thus, being tempted or even momentarily considering Satan's alluring deception is, by itself, not a sin. While Eve's demise began in her mind, it did not become sin until she took action.

Actions follow our thoughts. We may be able to hold off our actions for a certain length of time, but if we continue saturating our thoughts with the lies of this world rather than the truth of God's Word, we will eventually act accordingly. Our thoughts reflect our priorities and will eventually manifest in our decisions. Self-talk is usually self-prophecy. Today's thoughts lead to tomorrow's actions.

As mentioned previously, Adam was "with her" when all this transpired. He was a silent participant; the narrative mentions not a single word from him. This in itself is a major fail in both Adam and Eve. God created Adam first, and as the rest of Scripture bears out, He designed men to protect, love, and lead their wives and families.[8] Adam's silence doesn't go so far as being a sin (otherwise the fall would've occurred right then and there), but it most assuredly was unwise. Even though creation remained silent as Eve contemplated the serpent's lies, Adam shouldn't have. He should've intervened, reminded Eve of truth, reached out for her hand, and walked away with her.

But his thoughts were obviously in sync with Eve's, because when she offered the fruit to him, he also ate it. This was even more of an assault to God's created order. Adam used Eve as a guinea pig. Instead of being a man and eating it first to ensure that, if something terrible happened, Eve would remain safe and unharmed, Adam used her as a test dummy. He stood right there and watched her to see what would happen so he could make a more informed decision about eating the fruit himself. If she'd died on the spot, you can bet your bottom dollar he wouldn't have eaten it. But since she didn't, he followed his wife instead of following God and tasted the fruit.

In two swift bites, the briefest moment of time, both Adam and Eve chose to listen to Satan (whom they had no relationship with) instead of God, with whom they had walked intimately during their whole existence. They chose theory over truth, an appealing course of action over a proven, sure one. They let themselves be distracted from the reality and security of God's Word by entertaining notions of "higher thought" and an alternative interpretation. In their attempt to become wise, they became utter fools.

Unsurprisingly, the lie turned out to be…a lie. Adam and Eve's hope of becoming wise like God resulted in a "wisdom" they quickly realized they wanted no part of. They gained knowledge, but it was of death, despair, defeat, and desolation, not hope, intellect, eternal perception, and greatness. This realization was both instantaneous and long- term. It took mere seconds to grasp the gross error of their decision, but they'd live the rest of their lives witnessing how deep the poison of sin reached. Not one day would go by when they did not realize the lies of Satan had been just that— complete, outright, empty propaganda. The lies may have been dressed like royalty and even girded with some measure of truth. But in the end, they were pure deceit, designed to lead them away from God and corrupt the life and beauty He had intricately established in creation.

It's amazing how often we entertain new ideas, theories, philosophies, interpretations, and applications of Scripture that either borderline or blatantly contradict it. Then we're shocked when they turn out to be false (if we ever, in fact, come to that discovery). Unfortunately, our realizations aren't always instant, as Adam and Eve's were. We sometimes entertain deceitful thinking for days, weeks, even years before (if ever) discovering the error of our ways and turning back to truth. I believe a big part of this is because, unlike Adam and Eve, we are already fallen people living in a fallen world. When Adam and Eve sinned, it was a shock, because it was *the* introduction to sin in the world. The process leading to the sin was subtle, but once it happened, it acted as a direct affront to their entire beings and world around them. Contrarily, since we are already immersed in sin, its effects are not always immediately recognizable. The lies we choose to believe are so muddled by our already-sinful nature, it's difficult to determine where truth ends and lies begin. In other words, we're a hopeless mess, save for the grace of God.

What is God's grace? It's His Word. It's the Scripture leading up to Christ, it's Christ Himself as the incarnation of truth, and now it's the Holy Spirit, who helps us stay on track. Yet we have to do the work. Before truth can take effect in our lives and protect us from Satan's lies, we have to immerse ourselves in the Word. We must read it, listen to it, meditate on it, memorize it, talk about it, pray it, sing it. In other words, the Word needs to be the foundation upon which we think, act, believe, and hope. The more we saturate ourselves in God's Word, the more resistant we will be to the world's lies. We'll recognize them as lies more quickly, reject them outright, and offer council for others to do the same.

One final note before moving on to our last passage example. Believing lies and the disobedience that follows always leads to consequences. Adam and Eve experienced immediate consequences, yet they didn't realize the full extent of the ramifications for some time. Contrarily, we don't always see or experience the results of our disobedience. They may be subtle as the lies infect one area of our lives at a time. One day, however, we will stand before God, and everything will be laid bare before Him. Our sins will be exposed, and it will be excruciating. Just as Adam and Eve realized they were naked and tried to cover up, we'll be exposed to the degree of being naked and unable to cover up. Will we stand before Him with lives marked by humble reliance on His Word? Or will we look back with regret, realizing we thought ourselves above His Word and put it in subjection to us rather than the other way around? We'll all have regrets, but not all regrets will reflect the same degree of misplaced trust.

Jesus in the Wilderness

Jesus's temptation in the wilderness is a well-known account in the gospels and reveals more of Satan's deception techniques. Yet, where Adam and Eve were weak and caved to them, Jesus, in the midst of unfathomable physical weakness, stood firm and shut Satan down.

> Then Jesus was led up by the Spirit into the wilderness to be tempted by the devil. (Matthew 4:1)

The account preceding Jesus's temptation tells of His baptism and how God beautifully displayed favor upon Him—"the heavens were opened, and he saw the Spirit of God descending as a dove and lighting on Him, and behold, a voice out of the heavens said, 'This is My beloved Son, in whom I am well-pleased" (Matthew 3:16b–17). Jesus's baptism marked the beginning of His ministry, yet instead of immediately getting busy with teaching and healing, He headed toward desolation and temptation.

Whereas Satan approached Eve, the Spirit led Jesus to His place of temptation. Why? Several theories exist, but two stand out among them. First, Jesus was tempted in order to gain full understanding of the temptations we experience so He could relate to us more authentically as our Advocate (Hebrews 4:15). Second, His temptation meant He could begin His ministry by fully relying on the Spirit—something He would need to do every moment for the duration of His ministry on earth. The point for our study, however, is that Jesus's temptation was no accident. It was divinely ordained and planned—something that needed to happen before He could commence His formal ministry.

Upon entering the wilderness, He "…fasted forty days and forty nights, He then became hungry" (Matthew 4:2). Adam and Eve were tempted in the full comfort and luxury of the most perfect environment imaginable. They were well-fed, happy, and healthy. The Lord catered to their every whim. They lacked for nothing, literally having everything they could rightfully desire. The environment of Jesus's temptation, however, was drastically different. Geographically, He was surrounded by dry, barren land. Conversely, Adam and Eve lived in a lush garden and could reach out and eat plump, nutritious, satisfying vegetation. Jesus reached out and grasped fistfuls of sand, crumbling brush, and rock. He experienced the ramifications of their fall.

Jesus experienced drastic physical differences from Adam and Eve as well. Adam and Eve were fully hydrated and well-nourished in their absolute prime and strength. Jesus fasted forty days and forty nights. He was both dehydrated and famished. If you've never fasted (either by choice or circumstance), you have no idea how intense and damaging hunger can be. I struggled with an eating disorder for a long time. For years I deprived my body of proper nourishment, and it wreaked all kinds of physical and emotional havoc on me. Lacking proper hydration and nutrition depletes us not only of energy but also of the ability to focus, rest, think clearly, and cope with everyday setbacks. While clearly not with the same motivation, Jesus experienced similar results and was not in an optimal position for a spiritual battle with the devil. The Lord was incomprehensibly weak and forced to rely on the Spirit for spiritual and emotional nourishment, since He wasn't receiving it physically.

As we read in the Genesis account, Satan is not dumb. He waited for the perfect moment to approach Eve in the garden, when she was in eyesight of the tree of knowledge of good and evil. Likewise, when battling with Jesus, Satan waited for the most opportune moment—when Jesus was at His absolute weakest:

> And the tempter came and said to Him, "If You are the Son of God, command that these stones become bread." (Matthew 4:3)

Satan tempted Eve once. That was all it took for her and Adam to cave, and with a piece of fruit at that. This is especially disheartening, considering that they were inundated with other fruit all over the garden. Contrarily, Satan tempted Jesus three times. The first also targeted food, but it was far more distressing because of His physically weakened state. The first part of Satan's statement is rhetorical, since they both knew that Jesus was, in fact, the Son of God. But as with Eve, Satan's tactic was to cast doubt on God's identity and trustworthiness. The devil asked Eve a question, and here he cast doubt on Jesus's identity as God.

By questioning His identity, however, Satan tried to undermine not only Jesus's self-awareness, but also His ability to prove it ("command that these stones become bread"). By phrasing it this way, Satan linked Jesus's identity as God with His power, specifically His ability to transform dry desert stones into bread. This logic in reverse would indicate that, if Jesus can't make the stones into bread, then He isn't the Son of God.

The devil did his best to back Jesus into a corner—shrewdly, a corner that would satiate His intense physical hunger. More than that, Satan did it in a way that didn't seem like a big deal, nor would it seem like a sin for Jesus to do so. Just as he made light of God's word to Eve, he also made light of what would be a simple task for Jesus. After all, He would go on to transform water into wine and turn a very small quantity of bread and fish into a feast for thousands. Would it have been sinful for Him to transform a few stones into bread? Herein lies yet another deceitful tactic of Satan—action versus motivation. Is it inherently wrong for us to eat healthy, drink alcohol, buy nice things, or have a nice house? No. But those actions *can* be sinful if the motivations are selfish and ungodly. In this case, Jesus turning the stones into bread would have been sinful because He would've been doing it to acquiesce Satan. This is never acceptable, permissible, or wise. So what did He do instead?

> But He answered and said, "It is written, 'Man shall not live on bread alone, but on every word that proceeds out of the mouth of God.'" (Matthew 4:4)

Jesus is brilliant (which should surprise no one; He is, after all, God omniscient and incarnate). He didn't even entertain Satan's suggestion as Eve did. Instead, He spoke Scripture, accurately and punctually, into the situation. He combatted Satan's covert deception with God's overt truth. The Scripture He chose was no accident either. It's a quote from Deuteronomy 8 which, in its context, reads:

> "You shall remember all the way which the LORD your God has led you in the wilderness these forty years, that He might humble you, testing you, to know what was in your heart, whether you would keep His commandments or not. He humbled you and let you be hungry, and fed you with manna which you did not know, nor did your fathers know, that He might make you understand that man does not live by bread alone, but man lives by everything that proceeds out of the mouth of the LORD." (Deuteronomy 8:2–3)

This is so rich! The context of Jesus's quote is Moses's words to the Israelites who *wandered in the wilderness for forty years.* (Jesus has been in the wilderness for forty days.) They were intentionally left *hungry* (also like Jesus) in order to prove God's sufficiency in providing for them. (Once again, this is like Jesus now relying on the Spirit.) God was more than enough for every need of both the Israelites and Jesus— physically, emotionally, and spiritually. Wow, wow, wow! Unlike Eve, who added to God's Word, Jesus unleashed its full power by keeping it in its context and subsequently shutting the devil up about that temptation.

Despite Jesus's overwhelming victory against the devil's first temptation, Satan was not done with Him. This reveals his tenacity. We may be victorious over one of his temptations, but we should never grow pompous in a victory over Satan. The Apostle Peter warns Christians to "be of sober spirit, be on the alert. Your adversary, the devil, prowls around like a roaring lion, seeking someone to devour" (1 Peter 5:8). He is never content leaving the church alone, for he wants nothing more than to silence the gospel. Thus, it is not surprising that Satan tried to tempt Jesus again:

> Then the devil took Him into the holy city and had Him stand on the pinnacle of the temple, and said to Him, "If You are the Son of God, throw Yourself down; for it is written, 'He will command His angels concerning You'; and 'On their hands they will bear You up, So that You will not strike Your foot against a stone.'" (Matthew 4:5–6)

With this temptation, Satan upped his game and used the tactic the entirety of this book is trying to reveal: taking Scripture out of context is not only dangerous, but it also attacks and even cripples the advancement of the gospel in the world. Satan quoted Scripture to Jesus, trying to goad Him into doing what *he* wanted, not what *God* wanted. This passage is taken from Psalm 91:11–12, yet it is not considered a Messianic passage, meaning it was not written prophetically about Christ. In other words, God (and the Psalmist by extension) referred to believers, not to Christ, when He penned this passage. God is talking about how He will give angels charge over *us*, that He will guard *us* and bear *us* up so *we* won't strike *our* foot against a stone. Satan changed the object of the Psalm from believers in Christ to Jesus Himself.

In addition to being outrageously irresponsible with Scripture, this is an insult to Jesus. To exchange Jesus with His subjects is (crudely) like replacing the President of the United States with an illegal immigrant. Absolutely ridiculous. Yet, even more outlandish is that Satan thought he'd succeed. Did he really think Jesus, who authored Scripture, didn't remember that part? Or that He'd get confused about it?

For being awfully smart and cunning with Eve, Satan was awfully obtuse with Jesus. It's curious that this was the best Satan can do. Repeating Scripture erroneously back to Jesus is all he's got? He truly believed that was the best way to deceive Jesus into sin? Perhaps he depended far too much on Jesus's physically weakened state to override His ability to draw on His strength as deity. Or, perhaps he simply underestimated Jesus. Satan thinks quite highly of himself. So it wouldn't be surprising if, in his depraved mind, he truly thought he could outwit God Himself. Nevertheless, Satan should have known better than to go against God incarnate. He was delusional in thinking he could get the best of Him.

Once again, Jesus shut Satan down immediately with a verse taken in *proper* context:

> Jesus said to him, "On the other hand, it is written, 'You shall not put the LORD your God to the test'" (Matthew 4:7).

This verse is also taken from Deuteronomy, which states in full, "You shall not put the LORD your God to the test, as you tested Him at Massah" (Deuteronomy 6:16). As with Jesus's first response, knowing the context of the verse helps astronomically in realizing the force of Christ's words. (Satan knew the context of this verse. He knows Scripture better than any human on the planet. How else could he know how to twist it to serve his purposes?)

The most pressing question is, "What is Massah?" The answer is found in Exodus 17:1–7: an account of Israel complaining against God because they were thirsty. The people of Israel in the desert, angry over the lack of water, turned against Moses. (This happened numerous times.) Moses asked God what he should do, and God told him to strike the rock at Horeb and water will come out. Moses complied, the people drank, and Moses named the place Massah "because of the quarrel of the sons of Israel, and because they tested the LORD, saying, 'Is the LORD among us, or not?'" (Exodus 17:7).

Israel doubted God's presence, and Satan tried to get Jesus to doubt it too. With this temptation, Satan wanted to make Jesus prove God was with Him by throwing Himself down from the temple so God's angels would save Him. The devil's problem, however, was that he couldn't do it legitimately, for no verse in Scripture even remotely indicates that proof of God's presence is the ability to defy gravity. Thus, Satan *took Scripture out of context*, and Jesus responded with a passage that, in context, cut the heart out of the devil's crafty attempt.

When that temptation failed, Satan moved on to his final attempt:

> Again, the devil took Him to a very high mountain and showed Him all the kingdoms of the world and their glory; and he said to Him, "All these things I

will give You, if You fall down and worship me."
(Matthew 4:8–9)

This one is almost laughable. It seems more like a desperate
Hail Mary than a carefully crafted scheme. Satan realized he
couldn't use Scripture against its Author, so he moved to
straight incentive, telling Jesus to worship him, and he'll give
Him the world. The stupidity of Satan's proposal, however, is
that "the earth is the LORD's, and all it contains, the world,
and those who dwell in it" (Psalm 24:1). Jesus met Satan's
ridiculous request with a show of force. Satan may not be
finished with these temptations, but Jesus had reached His
limit:

> "Go, Satan! For it is written, 'You shall worship the LORD
> your God, and serve Him only.'" (Matthew 4:10)

I love how Jesus didn't even try to explain all the ways Satan's
request was stupid. He told him to leave, and as a passing
remark, He reminded Satan of one of the most basic,
foundational commands God has written: "You shall worship
the LORD your God, and serve Him only." Once again, this
quote is taken from Deuteronomy, but is a common theme
even in the Ten Commandments. There is only one God,
only one worthy of our hope, trust, loyalty, obedience, and
service.

Having thoroughly defeated Satan, "the devil left Him; and
behold, angels came and began to minister to Him." Ironic,
isn't it? The very thing Satan tempted Jesus to do (have angels
show up to help Him) is exactly what happens when Satan

leaves. Satan tried to deplete Jesus's spiritual steadfastness; angels came to build Him back up.

Before moving on to ways Satan specifically deceives people today (with parcels of truth wrapped in lies), let's conclude with some thoughts gleaned from both the creation and Jesus's temptation accounts. First, Satan cannot be trusted. Ever. He stands diametrically opposed to God in every way imaginable. Every word that comes out of his mouth is a lie, designed to lead us away from God. We need to shut him down with as much force as possible.

Second, by all accounts, Satan knows Scripture better than any human who has ever lived. In his epistle, James states, "You believe that God is one. You do well; the demons also believe, and shudder" (James 2:19). The reason Satan is so good at manipulating truth is because he knows truth better than his targets do. It's much easier to confuse and manipulate a child than an adult. Unfortunately, churches today are comprised of far too many spiritual infants instead of mature adults, making us easy targets for the wily attacks of the devil:

> For though by this time you ought to be teachers, you have need again for someone to teach you the elementary principles of the oracles of God, and you have come to need milk and not solid food. For everyone who partakes only of milk is not accustomed to the word of righteousness, for he is an infant. But solid food is for the mature, who because of practice have their senses trained to discern good and evil. (Hebrews 5:12–14)

We cannot fight Satan and his lies unless we are heavily armed with the truth of God's Word—not only understanding it, but immersing ourselves in it within its rightful context.

Third, we need to keep our guard up in every area of our lives in order to defend ourselves. Scriptural knowledge is by far the best armor we have, but we're also wise to invest in our physical, mental, and emotional states. Satan targets our weaknesses, as we observed both with Eve and Jesus's temptations. Satan didn't approach Eve until she was strategically positioned in sight of the tree, where he could lure her to it. With Jesus, he waited until He was in a physically weakened state and then made his first temptation about bread. We need to be aware of our weaknesses and build up extra defenses around them to ward off his attacks.

For example, say that we, like Eve, struggle with lusting after either sex or material possessions. To deal with sexual lust, we can install a number of programs on our computers, phones, and other devices that will block access to certain sites. Likewise, we can establish relationships with accountability partners who will check on us regularly and help keep us on the right path. With material possessions, we can set strict budgets, unsubscribe from tempting emails, magazines, or social media, and avoid going to retail establishments when it isn't necessary. We have a myriad of ways to bolster our defenses against Satan's attacks, and wise Christians will take any and all preventative measures necessary. As much as possible, we should refuse to put ourselves in vulnerable circumstances that make us easy targets. Jesus succeeded in refuting Satan, but we are most certainly not Jesus!

Fourth, we are wise to surround ourselves with a community of mature believers. Eve's community was Adam, and he failed miserably by not intervening on her behalf. Our closest relationships should be with those who are strong in faith and committed to Christ and who immerse themselves in truth. Obviously, we all stumble and err, but our most intimate community should be those who strive to walk in accordance with Scripture.

Fifth, *all* Scripture is inspired by God and profitable for teaching, reproof, correction, and training in righteousness (2 Timothy 3:16) and for shutting Satan up. Of all the "iconic" passages Jesus could have used to fight back against Satan, He chose to use passages from Deuteronomy—not exactly the most sought-after Bible study in Christian circles today. Yet by doing so, Jesus proved that every word of the Old Testament is God's Word, and that every word of Scripture is authoritative, powerful, and exactly what we need to fight Satan and his evil, gospel-denying schemes. We can take practical steps to provide extra measures of defense. But if we don't know, cherish, memorize, live by, and obey Scripture, we'll be as disoriented in our spiritual walks as a soldier separated from his platoon during battle.

Finally, since we will never have a direct conversation with Satan by which to be tempted, we need to be aware of how he works in and through our environment and relationships, so we can be on our guard. Two examples of his deceitful outworking in our lives are those of our current culture and media. Culture and media work hand in hand to promote every agenda under the sun except God's. They scream at us to follow our hearts, live our best lives now, do what feels right, and live by our own truth—all of which blatantly contradict God's Word, and thus, genuine Christian pursuits. Paul describes the situation brilliantly for those who have not yet come to faith in Christ:

> And you were dead in your trespasses and sins, in which you formerly walked according to the course of this world, according to the prince of the power of the air, of the spirit that is now working in the sons of disobedience. Among them we too all formerly lived in the lusts of our flesh, indulging the desires of the flesh and of the mind, and were by nature children of wrath, even as the rest. (Ephesians 2:1–3)

Satan's agenda is always death, and if he loses the war regarding our salvation, his secondary goal is to render our lives worthless in advancement of the gospel and the kingdom, so others remain dead. Our culture and the media are major weapons of Satan, "the prince and power of the air" (Ephesians 2:2), and he uses them to distract people from truth. Many people who think they're devout Christians are completely fooled by our media and culture. They compromise their faith and God's truth in an attempt to be "relevant" and loving to all people, thinking they're following in Jesus's footsteps. They don't realize they're treading fresh ground for the devil himself.

That is why this book exists—to challenge believers to understand God's Word, prioritize it as the central tenet of their life and faith, learn how Satan warps it into miserable lies that lead to our demise, and then take action against it by keeping God's Word in context in both study and personal application. The remaining chapters of this book will each target one myth—one lie Satan wields against the church under the guise of truth and love for humanity. We will pinpoint the myth, identify the truth within it, unpack the lies that have corrupted and taken the truth out of context, and then challenge ourselves to place the issue back within its proper context in Scripture, as well as in our hearts and lives.

Chapter Four
Judgment

Myth:

Jesus never judged people. He loved people equally, forgave without measure, and didn't criticize anyone, so we shouldn't either. Thus, "there must be no judging whatsoever...we must be easy, indulgent and tolerant, and allow almost anything for peace and quiet, and especially unity."[9]

The Truth Within the Myth:

Jesus did say things like, "Do not judge so that you will not be judged" (Matthew 7:1) and "God did not send His Son into the world to judge the world, but that the world might be saved through Him" (John 3:17).

Where Truth Gets Distorted by a Lie:

To be responsible "archeologists" of God's Word, we need to be willing and able to do some digging when something doesn't immediately make sense to us. At first glance, the liberal assertation that "Jesus never judged people, so we shouldn't either" seems true, based on the aforementioned Scriptures. However, it doesn't take a lot of scriptural knowledge to be aware of other passages like John 5:26–27, 30, which seem to contradict them:

> "For just as the Father has life in Himself, even so He gave to the Son also to have life in Himself; and He gave Him authority to execute judgement, because He is the Son of Man...I can do nothing on My own initiative. As I hear, I judge; and My judgment is just, because I do not seek My own will, but the will of Him who sent Me."

So which is it? Judge or don't judge? Did Jesus judge or didn't He? Or because there appears to be a contradiction, do we just throw out all of the Bible and reject everything we've known to be true?

The latter would be utter foolishness, because it's not a contradiction. If we probe a bit deeper, we realize there are different *types* of judgment. Jesus condemned one kind for us; He's not canceling any and all measures of judgment made by His people in this world. We'll begin our investigation about judgment with the passage from Matthew 7, determining how, when, and why we are supposed to judge others. Then we'll look into Jesus as Judge—how He did pass judgments on earth, and will do so again when He comes back.

Judgment as Discernment vs. Judgment as Condemnation

In Greek, the word for "judge" is *krino*. It has a range of meanings, from discerning to passing judgment to condemning. As English readers, we're at a disadvantage regarding the complexity and nuances of Greek words. Without doing a word study, we're left at the mercy of our English translations, which admittedly do their best, but are lacking if only because no two languages are 100 percent compatible.

Consider discrepancies even within our own language. Someone learning English may hear someone say, "That's so cool!" and understandably think the speaker is referring to temperature. Yet native English speakers understand the reference to indicate pleasure in something, not the temperature. When coming across a seemingly difficult or contradictory verse in Scripture, then, we must go deeper to understand the word first, then the context (immediate, book, and canon) of the verse it's in to bring clarity to the interpretation.

Since *krino* is a generally broad term, we must investigate the context in order to determine its precise meaning. Let's consider the verse from the Sermon on the Mount mentioned above:

> "Do not judge so that you will not be judged." (Matthew 7:1)

At first glance and without context, it would very much appear that Jesus prohibited any and all judgment of others—that we must permit and tolerate all actions and behavior if we are to avoid judgment ourselves. However, that is a grossly superficial interpretation of the text. Just five verses later Jesus wrote, "Do not give what is holy to dogs, and do not throw your pearls before swine, or they will trample them under their feet, and turn and tear you to pieces." How are we to determine the identity of dogs and swine without some measure of judgment and discernment? We can't!

Let's put this verse in the context of its familial passage, then:

> "Do not judge so that you will not be judged. For in the way you judge, you will be judged; and by your standard of measure, it will be measured to you. Why do you look at the speck that is in your brother's eye, but do not notice the log that is in your own eye? Or how can you say to your brother, 'Let me take the speck out of your eye,' and behold, the log is in your own eye? You hypocrite, first take the log out of your own eye, and then you will see clearly to take the speck out of your brother's eye. Do not give what is holy to dogs, and do not throw your pearls before swine, or they will trample them under their feet, and turn and tear you to pieces." (Matthew 7:1–6)

By way of (larger) context, this passage is a part of the Sermon on the Mount, which is Jesus's longest recorded sermon. He was speaking to His disciples (5:1–2), though we're not sure if that refers only to the twelve or those following Him in general. It's also possible that the crowds who previously followed Him eventually found Him and settled in to listen.

As with other sections in the Sermon on the Mount, Jesus began with a command, then He elaborated on the reasoning behind it. The command: don't judge. Why should we not judge? Because "in the way you judge, you will be judged." The latter judgment refers to God's judgment on us in the last days, when we will stand before Him and give an account for our lives and deeds (2 Corinthians 5:10). Thus, Jesus's instruction here doesn't refer to mere discernment or determination for purposes of accountability. *It means we should not judge for the purpose of condemnation—criticizing, shaming, and haughtily writing people off as if condemning them to hell.*

This conclusion is confirmed throughout the rest of the passage as Jesus used the example of a hypocrite pointing out the speck in his brother's eye when he has a log in his own. When we understand the historical context, particularly the religious climate of Jesus's day, this makes even more sense. The religious leaders (Pharisees, scribes, Sadducees, Herodians, etc.) were infamous for condemning others for any and every infraction. They acted as if they were God's specially appointed agents, as if He did their bidding upon request. If someone was sick or disabled, they concluded that it was the result of sin, either in his life or his parents' lives.[10] Consequently, they detested the ill and poor. They cared not for their souls; they wrote them off as hell-bound and couldn't care less about it. They hated entire nationalities of people simply because of their ethnicity. They disrespected women and viewed them with disdain. They were arrogant and showed off their "holiness" by praying elaborate prayers crafted to shame and intimidate the poor or uneducated.

Their entire existence was marked by condemnation—they cared only about their status and shunned those who disrupted their misguided pursuits.

We see these leaders' hypocrisy on numerous levels, but primarily because they, who claimed to be righteous and closest to God, showed by their actions just how far they were from Him. Worse, they ostracized others and stunted their faith by making demands that were nearly impossible to keep. They were, in essence, acting as "gods" and lording their status, wealth, and piety over anyone and everyone they could. In their haste of condemning others for minor flaws, they overlooked the gross sins that consumed their own lives: pride, self-deceit, and hate, all worthy of far greater damnation.

Jesus called out their hypocrisy and the hypocrisy of any who followed them. He said that if we want to judge others in order to condemn them on earth, then one day we will be judged by the One who actually has authority to condemn us to hell eternally.

Yet notice the shift Jesus took in verse five. He told them they should "first take the log out of your own eye, and then you will see clearly to take the speck out of your brother's eye." While He still chastised condemning judgment, He didn't say to avoid *any and every* kind of judgment. He rather prescribed a method for properly judging others for purposes of *discernment and edification.*

First, He instructed the original hearers (and us, by extension) to remove the logs from their own eyes. We're never in a position to discern anything in others until we're first well aware of, and subsequently repentant of, our own sins and pitfalls. To put it another way, we're to judge ourselves first. We should be intimately familiar with and actively repenting of our own failures before noticing the failures of others. There's no magic formula, but my own rule of thumb when I'm attempting to discern something in someone else is to ask, "When is the last time God convicted *me* of something? Have I repented and turned away from that and toward God?" Then I question my motivation. "Did I notice this in an attempt to make myself look better or because I love them and genuinely want what's best for them?" When I can answer these questions satisfactorily, I've entered a more humble and Spirit-filled state.

Also, when we're consistently being sharpened ourselves, we tend to be more loving, forgiving, and gracious to others. This is the second part of Jesus's instruction. After removing our own logs, we can "see clearly to take the speck out of your brother's eye." In other words, *we are supposed to see and then remove the speck for others.* That's how we put love into action. If someone literally had something in their eye and was unable to get it out or didn't have access to a mirror, of course we would offer a hand and take a look. Naturally, we couldn't do this with a log wedged in our own eye. But if we're free and clear, we're supposed to help others get the muck out of theirs. Or another example: if someone needed assistance brushing dirt off the back of their shirt, we wouldn't be of much help if our hands were covered in mud, right? We need to get clean before we can help others do the same. But make no mistake. We're supposed to help others as well.

The method in which we do this is crucial, however. Instead of hastily jumping to conclusions and writing people off (condemning judgment), we're to act with gentleness and care. Again, taking the metaphor literally, we would never jab our fingers in someone's eye in order to remove a mere speck of dust. Rather, we would examine the situation, determine where the speck is, and then gently remove it to the best of our ability.

Therein lies the repeating mantra of this book—context. Not only is context important for interpreting and applying Scripture, but context is also crucial for properly judging the actions of those around us. Determining the identity and location of the speck is imperative before removing it. So is determining the context of the actions/behaviors we discern in others. Far more often than not, when we see or hear of someone erring, we don't have all the information. We see one action in one moment of time (unless we'd been spying on them or something, which would be weird). Even if the action was horrible, chances are we don't know what's really going on, have no idea what led to the action, and don't understand their heart or motivation. It may have been one weak moment as opposed to the culmination of a concerning trend. Before jumping to conclusions, we should conduct due diligence and place the action and/or behavior within its appropriate context.

How do we go about that? Jesus conveniently gave us a gentle and loving way to do exactly that:

> "If your brother sins, go and show him his fault in private; if he listens to you, you have won your brother.

> But if he does not listen to you, take one or two more with you, so that by the mouth of two or three witnesses every fact may be confirmed. If he refuses to listen to them, tell it to the church; and if he refuses to listen even to the church, let him be to you as a Gentile and a tax collector." (Matthew 18:15–17)

Once again, Jesus spoke and taught His disciples in this passage. The first observation worth noting is that the person at fault is a brother—a fellow believer. It's crucial that we understand this, both in our judgment discussion and in this restoration one because *only believers and fellow disciples of Christ are subjected to church discernment and discipline.* Nonbelievers are not held to the same standards we are. While we should encourage godly living and aim to show its timeless wisdom to everyone, it's not our job to judge, critique, or correct people outside the faith. We lovingly discipline brothers and sisters, not strangers:

> But actually, I wrote to you not to associate with any so-called brother if he is an immoral person, or covetous, or an idolater, or a reviler, or a drunkard, or a swindler—not even to eat with such a one. For what have I to do with judging outsiders? Do you not judge those who are within the church? But those who are outside, God judges. Remove the wicked man from among yourselves. (1 Corinthians 5:11–13)

Aside from confirming once again that Christians are *supposed* to judge each other with the ultimate goal of loving accountability, the Apostle Paul also confirmed that we are to focus only on other believers. The church has more than enough issues to keep us completely occupied. We need to leave judgment for "outsiders" in God's hands.

Back to our Matthew 18 passage. Once we determine/confirm that the person in question is a self-proclaimed Christian, we need to clarify and organize our observations and the faults in his (or her) behavior. Jesus asserts the culprit has, in fact, sinned, yet sometimes in our experience, that's more of an assumption than a fact. Again, the Pharisees judged the sick and disabled, assuming their calamity was the result of sin. They jumped to conclusions. We are not at liberty to do the same.

As Matthew 18 prescribes, if our brother has sinned (or it really appears as if he has), we need to have a private conversation with him. Only in this private conversation do we reveal the sin we've witnessed. The seclusion of this conversation is imperative for several reasons. First, at this point, it's no one else's business. If the brother's fall was a one-time mistake and he's genuinely repentant and wants to make amends, there would be zero benefit from anyone else (except potentially harmed bystanders) being privy to his error. In fact, it could be detrimental. People could jump to conclusions and wrongfully judge him condemningly, casting unnecessary shame and guilt where none is due.

Privacy in this conversation is also crucial to keep defenses down and maintain a loving, gentle, non-condemning environment. Except for situations in which the Holy Spirit had already convicted and drawn us to repentance, we automatically tend to get defensive when facing accusations of any kind. These defenses are greatly exacerbated by a hostile or public environment. Thus, we must orchestrate and maintain a secluded, loving atmosphere for these confrontational conversations.[11]

If the brother listens and repents, the goal has been achieved, and everyone should celebrate. But if he refuses to listen, Jesus advised us to "take one or two more with you, so that by the mouth of two or three witnesses every fact may be confirmed." Notice the continued element of privacy—only one or two additional individuals are brought in at this point. While not specified here, it's recommended that these individuals be specifically chosen, not just some random friends. In fact, it would be wise to include a pastor/elder/leader in the church, as well as someone the erring brother respects and admires. The point of this conversation is to go "on record" while maintaining an air of seclusion.

If the brother still refuses to listen, at that point the matter should be told "to the church." This step makes the sin public knowledge, not for the sake of condemnation, but for the sake of accountability and corporate discipline as determined by the ruling elders, pastor, or leadership of a church. Church discipline is a rare practice nowadays, to our shame. We are far too tolerant of sin, too accepting of moral failure. If the church is what God created it to be—a family—then discipline must be implemented so restoration, healing, and growth can occur. Just as we cannot raise godly (or even decent) children without discipline, neither can the church raise up godly Christians without implementing discipline and correction when necessary.

If taking it public doesn't change the brother's heart, then Jesus says, "'Let him be to you as a Gentile and a tax collector'" (verse 17). Now, Jesus is not saying to treat them poorly, write them off, neglect, ridicule, or shame them. Rather, He is saying to treat them as we are supposed to treat unbelievers— to love and speak truth to them with gentleness and respect, for the sake of winning them to Christ (or back to Him, in this instance).

Thus concludes the method of approaching a brother (or sister) who is living in sin. We are absolutely supposed to judge situations and actions of our fellow brethren in Christ, for that's the only way we can sharpen each other and offer godly accountability to one another. But this judgment is not that of condemnation. It's not done in disdain for or apathy toward our brother's spiritual state. Rather, it's a judgment of humble love—of discernment for the purposes of edification, sanctification, and restoration when necessary.

Jesus Did Judge Others; He Is the Ultimate Judge

The claim that Jesus didn't judge others is, frankly, preposterous. He not only issued judgments while He was on earth, but He will also act as our final judge in the last days. While there are dozens of references to both timeframes of His judgment, we will explore only a few passages for each.

Jesus made judgments against people, specifically the scribes and the Pharisees, during His ministry on earth. One particularly potent passage is found in Matthew 23 and is traditionally labeled "The Eight Woes":

76

"But woe to you, scribes and Pharisees, hypocrites, because you shut off the kingdom of heaven from people; for you do not enter in yourselves, nor do you allow those who are entering to go in. Woe to you, scribes and Pharisees, hypocrites, because you devour widows' houses, and for a pretense you make long prayers; therefore you will receive greater condemnation. Woe to you, scribes and Pharisees, hypocrites, because you travel around on sea and land to make one proselyte; and when he becomes one, you make him twice as much a son of hell as yourselves…Woe to you, scribes and Pharisees, hypocrites! For you tithe mint and dill and cummin, and have neglected the weightier provisions of the law: justice and mercy and faithfulness; but these are the things you should have done without neglecting the others. You blind guides, who strain out a gnat and swallow a camel! Woe to you, scribes and Pharisees, hypocrites! For you clean the outside of the cup and of the dish, but inside they are full of robbery and self-indulgence…Woe to you, scribes and Pharisees, hypocrites! For you are like whitewashed tombs which on the outside appear beautiful, but inside they are full of dead men's bones and all uncleanness. So you, too, outwardly appear righteous to men, but inwardly you are full of hypocrisy and lawlessness." (excerpts from Matthew 23:13–28)

If that is not judgment, I'm not sure what is. These were harsh, fierce words spoken against people who were typically "off-limits" and considered above reproach. Jesus, however, targeted them for their hypocrisy and judged not only their actions, but also their hearts. Also noteworthy is the fact that Jesus did not proclaim these statements in private; He spoke them to crowds of people, along with His disciples. So this was not only judgment. It was also public condemnation (which He could do, because He is, in fact, God). He absolutely judged people for their actions and behaviors during His ministry on earth.

While this was clearly a judgment of condemnation, Jesus also judged people via discernment and divine insight. For example, at one time during his ministry, some men picked up their paralyzed friend's bed and took it—with their friend in it—to Jesus. Noting the friends' faith, Jesus told the paralytic, "Son, your sins are forgiven" (Mark 2:5). Some scribes were present and thought, "This fellow blasphemes" because only God can forgive sins, and they were far from convinced that Jesus was God. Even though they didn't say so out loud, Jesus, "knowing their thoughts said, 'Why are you thinking evil in your hearts?'"[12] Jesus judged what was in their unbelieving, arrogant hearts. He knew what they were thinking, just as He knew that Judas Iscariot would betray Him. He also knows the innermost thoughts in our hearts today. Jesus judged others in every sense of the word, from discernment to condemnation.

After reading these examples, one might be tempted to argue that Jesus judged only the religious hypocrites, not the "sinners," poor, sick, or downtrodden. But that's not true either. In fact, He announced judgment on entire cities:

Then he began to denounce the cities in which most of His miracles were done, because they did not repent. "Woe to you, Chorazin! Woe to you, Bethsaida! For if the miracles had occurred in Tyre and Sidon which occurred in you, they would have repented long ago in sackcloth and ashes. Nevertheless I say to you, it will be more tolerable for Tyre and Sidon in the day of judgment than for you. And you, Capernaum, will not be exalted to heaven, will you? You will descend to Hades; for if the miracles had occurred in Sodom which occurred in you, it would have remained to this day. Nevertheless I say to you that it will be more tolerable for the land of Sodom in the day of judgment, than for you." (Matthew 11:20–24)

These cities were not holy, sacred places reserved for the religious elite. They were normal cities and villages, full of normal, regular people who refused to believe just as much as the Pharisees and scribes did. Let that sink in. Jesus judged non-religious people—rich, poor, and everyone between.

One of the biggest buzzwords in our culture today is "oppressed." Many think that white people (particularly men) are oppressors, while people of a different color or gender are the oppressed. This logic is faulty for many reasons that we don't have time to dive into now, but one consequence of this thinking is that, in their minds, the "oppressed" cannot be held responsible for anything. Indeed, even if they sin/break the law, it's not *really* their fault. It's the fault of the white man who oppressed them in the first place.

A recent news story highlights this logic in action. A Minneapolis mother, Arabella Foss-Yarbrough, was making dinner for her children one evening when a neighbor, who had allegedly been harassing her for months, began shooting into her apartment. She called the police, who ended up using deadly force on the suspect because he was still firing his weapon. Later, protestors showed up at her apartment in defense of the suspect because he was black and allegedly had mental health issues. When trying to reenter her apartment, Arabella defended herself and her children against the protesters with statements like, "That man intentionally tried to kill us," that there are bullet "casings in the hallway…the shot went through my door to the pillar in the kitchen; I was cooking food for my kids." She continued, "you all should've came and helped him when he was alive…my kids have to see you guys celebrate a man who tried to kill them."[13]

Black Lives Matter protesters yelled back in defense of the suspect because, in their minds, his death was the police's fault. They didn't think the suspect should've been shot. It apparently didn't matter that the suspect had fired multiple shots into the apartment, attempting to kill both Arabella and her two young children, who, ironically, are also black. In the BLM mindset, black people are oppressed and cannot be held responsible for their actions, criminal or otherwise. They supposedly need reparations, not reprimands; pardon, not punishment.

Whereas some try to nuance select and decontextualized verses to fit this agenda, Scripture is abundantly clear on the subject: *Jesus shows no partiality*. The Pharisees and scribes are easy to dislike because of their arrogance and condemning attitudes. But everyone else (you and me included) is just as guilty as they. Despite wanting to cheer for the underdog and assume that disadvantaged (real or perceived) people have excuses for their behavior, *no one is without excuse.* All have sinned and fall short of God's glory (Romans 3:23), and the wages of every sin is death (Romans 6:23a). Jesus judged the lack of belief of both the religious elite and the downtrodden. A person's societal status, skin color, zip code, occupation, gender, church attendance record, and financial portfolio have zero bearing on their status with God.

Part of Jesus's aforementioned judgment was directed to the future, which reveals the second component of His role as Judge—the last days. One passage confirming Jesus's ultimate judgeship is also particularly applicable to our topic in this book. It's found in one of Apostle Paul's letters to Timothy, his mentee and "child in the faith":

> I solemnly charge you in the presence of God and of *Christ Jesus, who is to judge the living and the dead,* and by His appearing and His kingdom: preach the word; be ready in season and out of season; reprove, rebuke, exhort, with great patience and instruction. For the time will come when they will not endure sound doctrine; but wanting to have their ears tickled, they will accumulate for themselves teachers in accordance with their own desires, and will turn away their ears from the truth and will turn aside to myths. (2 Timothy 4:1–4, emphasis added)

Jesus Christ will judge everyone in the last days with the ultimate judgment of either condemnation or mercy, depending on what people believed on earth. Those who believe in and place their faith in Him are covered by His sacrifice on the cross and granted access to eternity with Him. Those who refuse—who reject His offer of salvation through His gospel—will be judged according to their sin, the consequence of which is eternity enduring God's wrath in hell.

Not only *did* Jesus judge, but Jesus also *is* the ultimate Judge. Obviously, we are not Jesus and do not have His authority. But we are absolutely called to follow Him as we judge our brothers and sisters in the faith for the purpose of correction, edification, and sanctification.

Notice what Paul told Timothy in the passage above—the motivation for Timothy to be godly is *because* of God's authority and Christ's impending final judgment. Because the final judgment is coming, the apostles were charged with advancing the gospel and growing God's kingdom as much as possible on earth. The physical universe is on a clock, and only God knows when the time will be up.

It's not popular to talk about God's judgment and wrath in our culture. In fact, it's taboo. All we want to hear about is love, acceptance, and approval of our every decision. We want to feel affirmed, not convicted; praised, not scathed. And far too many preachers gladly acquiesce. Sermons today sound more like self-help sessions than self-denying ones, and the only thing accomplished is getting people further from Christ. George

Whitefield once said, "It is a poor sermon that gives no offense; that neither makes the hearer displeased with himself nor with the preacher." Why? Because "the word of God is living and active and sharper than any two-edged sword, and piercing as far as the division of soul and spirit, of both joints and marrow, and able to judge the thoughts and intentions of the heart" (Hebrews 4:12). Scripture is truth, and some truth, like the coming judgment, is hard to hear. But it's worth the temporary discomfort of conviction if it helps us to avoid the coming permanent torture if we ignore it.

Jesus judged on earth and will judge again in the final days. That reality doesn't change or go away just because we don't like it. We're in no position to remove a single verse from Scripture, strip it of its context, and twist it like a pretzel until it conforms to our ideologies. The Lord will hold us accountable to truth, whether we believe it or not. When we stand before Jesus one day, He's not going to say, "Oh! You didn't realize the truth? My bad for not manifesting myself in human form again and inviting you to coffee so I could share it with you face to face. That's on Me. Open the gates, Peter, and let this one in!" Why won't He say that? *Because He has made the truth clear in His Word.* He's given us ample evidence of truth in creation and tons of undiluted truth in His Word. If we get it wrong, it's because *we* are irresponsible—too lazy, deceived, or apathetic to put in the time and effort to get it right.

In all our attempts to avoid judgment on ourselves and others, we neglect to realize the most fundamental gospel truth about the subject. Yes, Jesus made judgments while on earth, and yes,

He will be the final judge in the last days. But fundamentally, we must realize that we are already judged because we placed ourselves under God's wrath long ago:

> For God did not send His Son into the world to judge the world, but that the world might be saved through Him. He who believes in Him is not judged; *he who does not believe has been judged already, because he has not believed in the name of the only begotten Son of God. This is the judgment, that the Light has come into the world, and men loved the darkness rather than the Light,* for their deeds were evil. For everyone who does evil hates the Light, and does not come to the Light for fear that his deeds will be exposed. But he who practices the truth comes to the Light, so that his deeds may be manifested as having been wrought in God. (John 3:17–21, emphasis added)

Apart from Christ, we stand condemned in our sin. Only believing in Jesus Christ and His gospel can save us and render us safe instead of doomed in the final judgment. There is "salvation in no one else; for there is no other name under heaven that has been given among men by which we must be saved" (Acts 4:12). Yet here's the kicker: we cannot make His name anything we want it to be. We cannot turn on a puny, battery-operated tea-light candle and claim it's the blinding glory of God's radiance simply because it's easier to handle.

Salvation, true Light, is available only when we step into the Light on His terms. We are in no position to negotiate. It's either Christ's salvation or eternal damnation.

As Christians, we are not merely responsible for ourselves, however. While we are ultimately responsible for our choices and actions, we also bear responsibility in the lives of those around us. God chose to make us a family; a family is how we must act. Thus, while it may seem safe or easier to avoid judging other believers (via discernment for the sake of mutual sanctification), neglecting to do so results in disobedience to God and His Word. Further, refusing to judge others doesn't exempt us from God's judgment. Jesus will not commend us for "staying in our own lane" when we witness sin in His family and refuse to do anything about it. That's like seeing our neighbor's house on fire and saying, "I'm sure they have it under control" and then going about our business. We would never do that! We'd call the fire department, run every hose we could find, and even rush in to try to save them if at all possible.

The same is true for sin within the church. Jesus instructs us to love others, which inevitably includes noticing sin and struggles they may be working through. And He gives us what we need to conquer it, both in our lives and in the lives of others around us, through the prescribed method detailed in Matthew 18. Why? Because final judgment is coming. We don't love each other if we don't do everything possible to drag people out of hell with the gospel—both positionally in Christ through salvation and practically through sanctification in our lives. When we listen to Satan's lies, advocating that sin should be ignored under the guise of "being non-judgmental," we watch them burn while holding a hose.

To conclude, judgment is not only permitted. It's also required for believers in Jesus Christ. Jesus judged while He was on earth, and he'll judge again in the final days, when we all stand before Him and are held accountable for our actions and choices. His judgments were both of discernment and condemnation, for He had the authority and power to execute both. We, as His followers, do not have (and shouldn't want) authority for condemnation, and therefore should never judge for the sake of damnation. But we do have the authority and responsibility to discern sin in the lives of our fellow believers. We must not do this for the purpose of attacking, but rather for the purpose of conviction, restoration, and furthered sanctification in each other's lives. If we love one another, we will intervene when we notice sins, because we know God's final judgment is coming. We love them too much to let them flounder, unaware of their condition. Judgment is a natural, necessary aspect of sanctification, and one we must embrace (properly, according to God's Word) if we are to grow in His image and toward our ultimate goal of glorifying and enjoying Him forever.

Chapter Five

Love

Myth:

Jesus loved first and foremost. His love is the fundamental attribute of His character. This means He accepted everyone and every decision they made. In other words, love wins. It triumphs over all else.

The Truth Within the Myth:

Jesus absolutely loved people during His ministry on earth, just as He loves people fiercely today.

Where Truth Gets Distorted by a Lie:

A Misunderstanding of Biblical Love

Love is one of the most overused, abused, misunderstood, and flimsy words in the English language and culture. It is a word we have destroyed—defining and redefining ad nauseam. By attributing so many meanings to it, we have rendered it powerless. Any sacredness and purity that gave it weight in generations past have seemingly evaporated like a mist in the storms our culture has raged with its thorough lack of understanding. I have no doubt this is of Satan's doing. The further he can remove biblical definitions from language, the more successful he becomes in interfering with God's gospel initiative.

Only the Holy Spirit can change the minds of those outside the faith. But Christians should define love as we do anything else—through the lens of God's Word. We must be careful how we use every word, lest we aid in its distortion and lead people (ourselves foremost) further from God and His truth. We must sift through the cultural muck and mire like archeologists to discover and cling to truth as God defines them.

So what is love?

Sometimes it's helpful to begin a definition by eliminating errors that have arisen over the years. I specifically want to address these because they reveal lies that Satan has managed to weave into people's definitions of love. If Satan can redefine terms, particularly in ways that contradict God's Word, he can wreak havoc on society. And that's precisely what he's done with love. He's convinced people that love is more about whims and self-gratification than truth and God. This has had devastating results in our families and culture.

Lies we need to debunk, then, begin with this: love is not a feeling or emotion. While we do experience emotions when we love someone, love is not based on our feelings. "Follow your heart" and "do what feels right" are some of the worst pieces of anti-biblical, anti-Jesus advice that exists. In the train of our beings, our emotions are (and should be) the caboose. They follow our brains and beliefs for a reason—they make horrendous navigators and leaders.

Secondly, love is not temporary. Feelings are temporary; they go wherever the wind takes them. Love, however, is not. This means it's not possible to "fall" either in or out of love. Love is not a sparkling, effervescent pink pond stirred by Cupid that people can fall into and then crawl out of when the bubbles of infatuation have fizzled out. Consequently, love is also not fluid. We do not just happen to love whoever we're floating closest to in Cupid's pool, then drift over to someone else and start loving them instead. (Even though most romantic comedies and novels would lead us to believe otherwise).

Further, love is not lust. It is not the emotional or physical erection (we're all adults here) one gets when they see an attractive person. Love based on physical attraction won't last much longer than the Botox used to garner it.

Love is also not conditional. It doesn't depend upon a recipient's compatibility or ability or willingness to reciprocate. The best human example of this is parents' love for their children. It matters not that children drain their parents' emotions, energy, finances, and even sanity and hardly, if ever, replenish the coffers they've spent their lives depleting. Good parents love their children fiercely without expecting anything in return.

In line with our parenting example, love is not easy. We can't expect immediate or even positive results of loving. Emotions can change from gushy infatuation to intense loathing in a matter of moments. Hoping to have an easy ride for a lifetime is as much a fantasy as a unicorn.

Love is also not synonymous with acceptance or approval. To love someone does not mean to accept or approve of everything about them, nor everything they say and do. I love my daughters unconditionally, but not a day goes by when I accept or approve of their every action, word, or behavior. In fact, I reprove and correct their erroneous, sinful ways *because* I love them—because my husband and I want them to live fully, love Jesus, and experience the most joy, peace, and contentment possible.

Lastly, despite the world attempting to define it in countless ways, love cannot be understood apart from God.

Defining Biblical Love

Now let's shift our focus from what love is not to what love is. Its complexity renders it impossible to define comprehensively and succinctly, but here's a working definition gleaned from Scripture:

> *Love is an active, constant attribute of God embodied perfectly in the Trinity as He relates to Himself—a selfless commitment and dedication to the well-being, edification, and glorification of each member to one another. Since we are His image bearers on earth, love is gifted to us as both*

90

an intrinsic part of our spiritual DNA and a choice of obedience to both God and fellow man. To love someone is to seek their good purposefully, consistently, and sacrificially as defined by God and purposed for His glory.

First, God

Foremost and above all, we must recognize that love is an attribute of God. We wouldn't experience it or even know it existed without Him. The world has polluted it, but its origin lies in the One who created the world. It's an integral part of His character, and one He graciously allows us to partake in and experience. We find one of the most iconic passages revealing this attribute in 1 John:

> Beloved, let us love one another, for love is from God; and everyone who loves is born of God and knows God. The one who does not love does not know God, for God is love. By this the love of God was manifested in us, that God has sent His only begotten son into the world so that we might live through Him. In this is love, not that we loved God, but that He loved us and sent His Son to be the propitiation for our sins. (1 John 4:7–10)

Biblical Greek had three words for love: *eros, philia,* and *agape. Eros* refers to erotic or sexual love/passion, *philia* refers to brotherly love, and *agape* refers to a deeper meaning of love— "a steadfast, unselfish concern for the welfare of the other person."[14] This third love, agape, is the one used most frequently when referring to God and is used in this passage from 1 John.

John reveals and confirms not only that "love is from God," but that "God is love." We must exercise caution with this phrase, however, because while John offers an explanation, it's not a definition. Love is a central and undeniable *part* of God's identity, but it is not the entirety of His identity. Nor are love and God synonymous (i.e., while God is love, love is not God).

> Equating love with God is a major mistake which has produced much unsound religious philosophy and has brought forth a spate of vaporous poetry completely out of accord with the Holy Scriptures and altogether of another climate from that of historic Christianity... f literally God is love, then literally love is God, and we are all duty bound to worship love as the only God there is. If love is equal to God then God is only equal to love, and God and love are identical. Thus we destroy the concept of personality in God and deny outright all His attributes save one, and that one we substitute for God.[15]

Therefore, God is love in that He perfectly embodies and manifests the ultimate, purest form of love in existence. Love comprises the essence of His being and how He relates to Himself and the world. And it can be argued that love motivates everything He does—every decision He makes and action He takes, including sending Jesus to earth to die on the cross for our sins. But He is not synonymous with love. We do not worship love as God; we worship God, who is the manifestation of love.

Love is from God and is an intrinsic part of God's identity, but it would be meaningless if it was not active. Like other divine attributes shared with humanity, love must be put into action to be fully realized. It's first put into action within the Trinity. By actively and constantly exercising love toward one another, the members of the Trinity reveal its nature and how their creation should live it out: through relationships. We can theorize, postulate, and philosophize about love all day long. But we experience it only when we put it in the context of relationships. This is what the Trinity reveals to us. The love among the Father, Son, and Holy Spirit is not some stagnant posture of theory. It's an active reality that forms the basis for the way we should relate to one another.

Trinitarian love is witnessed clearly in Scripture, most prominently between the Father and Son (Jesus):

> The glory which You have given Me I have given to them, that they may be one, just as We are one; I in them and You in Me, that they may be perfected in unity, so that the world may know that You sent Me, and loved them, even as You have loved Me. Father, I desire that they also, whom You have given Me, be with me where I am, so that they may see My glory which You have given Me, for You loved Me before the foundation of the world. (John 17:22–23, 24b)

Unity between the Father and Son is inseparable from and fueled by the love they have for one another. Jesus abided in His Father's love (John 15:10) during His earthly ministry, which reflected the love they had experienced (and still do) with one another from eternity past. The Trinity is the most holy, pure example of a loving relationship that we have, and while references to the Holy Spirit are not as frequent, we do witness the loving relationship among all three in Jesus's baptism:

> After being baptized, Jesus came up immediately from the water; and behold, the heavens were opened, and he saw the Spirit of God descending as a dove and lighting on Him, and behold, a voice out of the heavens said, "This is My beloved Son, in whom I am well-pleased." (Matthew 3:16–17)

Despite being the most silent member of the Trinity, evidence of the Holy Spirit and His love for the Father and Son is evident. Further, love in humanity is a fruit of the Spirit— "The fruit of the Spirit is love, joy, peace, patience..." (Galatians 5:22). God can't give love if He doesn't first know and experience it. Thus, the Trinity—Father, Son, and Holy Spirit—embodies love actively within their relationships with one another.

One more crucial component to love is its consistency and steadfastness—it is unwavering, unchanging, and constant, just as God is. In Malachi, God states, "I, the Lord, do not change" (Malachi 3:6). Likewise, the author of Hebrews declares, "Jesus Christ is the same yesterday and today and forever" (Hebrews 13:8). If God doesn't change, neither does His love. His love never fails (1 Corinthians 13:8).

Part of this steadfastness is commitment. When God decides to love someone, He honors that commitment over and over again. Take Israel, for example. They failed God more times than it's possible to count. Reading through the Old Testament is like hitting your head against a brick wall—they just can't seem to get it! They cannot bring themselves to honor and be loyal to Him, despite everything He'd done for them. And yet, God never relents on His commitment to them. He punishes, banishes, exiles, and allows them to be defeated by their enemies, but He never removes His love and commitment from them:

> For the LORD will not abandon His people, nor will He forsake His inheritance. (Psalm 94:14)

> Who will separate us from the love of Christ? Will tribulation, or distress, or persecution, or famine, or nakedness, or peril, or sword?…For I am convinced that neither death, nor life, nor angels, nor principalities, nor things present, nor things to come, nor powers, nor height, nor depth, nor any other created thing, will be able to separate us from the love of God, which is in Christ Jesus our Lord. (Romans 8:35, 38–39)

This commitment reveals and leads to the ultimate purpose of love (and everything else in life), which is to glorify God. It is to lift His name high, exalt Him, and ascribe Him utmost worth, honor, and praise. As strange as it may sound, God glorifies Himself and did so long before He created the universe. While self-glorification is a completely selfish endeavor for us, it's quite the opposite for God because His glorification reflects His unmatched holiness. Only He knows just how magnificent, beautiful, and awe-inspiring He is. He is the only One in the universe actually worthy of worship! Finite, created beings can never comprehend or exhaust His glory, which is why He first glorifies Himself and then invites us to do the same. The more we glorify God by loving and obeying Him, the more we will realize just how truly stunning He is. And this will be an eternity-long endeavor, for even beings who are in His presence nonstop can't get used to His glory:

> I saw the Lord sitting on a throne, lofty and exalted, with the train of His robe filling the temple. Seraphim stood above Him, each having six wings: with two he covered his face, and with two he covered his feet, and with two he flew. And one called out to another and said, "Holy, holy, holy, is the Lord of hosts, the whole earth is full of His glory." And the foundations of the thresholds trembled at the voice of him who called out, while the temple was filling with smoke. (Isaiah 6:1–4)

Seraphim, who are in God's presence all the time, still cannot bear even to look at Him because of His holiness and glory. They chant and sing honor and praises to Him nonstop, and that is but the tiniest glimpse of the adoration He deserves. He really is *that* amazing, and only He fully knows the depths of His awesomeness. He's also the only one who knows how incomplete we are if we don't recognize and advance His glory in our own lives. His love, a fundamentally defining attribute of His being, is an integral part of His glory. Best of all, He doesn't keep it to Himself. He alone knows the full power, beauty, and purity of love, but He invites humanity to partake in it. For reasons completely lost on me, He decided not only to love us, but to allow us to experience love as well.

Love for God

With this we move to the second part of our definition about love originating in the Trinity:

> *Since we are His image bearers on earth, He gives love to us as both an intrinsic part of our spiritual DNA and a choice we commit to making to God and our fellow man. To love someone is to seek their good purposefully, consistently, and sacrificially, as defined by God and purposed for His glory.*

When God created humans, He did so in His image, in His likeness (Genesis 1:26–27). He built the capacity to love within the very essence of our beings, just as it is the essence of His. What a gift! Think about it. God didn't have to create anything. He is perfectly whole, complete, content, and without any need or unmet desire. Yet He decided to share His glory, goodness, and love with other beings. He wanted to let others in on His majesty, so He created beings in His likeness—beings with spirits capable of exemplifying His character traits and attributes.

The gift of love has been endowed to every human being who has ever lived. God designed love to be experienced and exercised in a particular manner. Therefore, love is supposed to be divinely reciprocal. Love is not first a horizontal endeavor among humanity; it is first to be directed vertically toward God. We were created to recognize and return God's love:

> We love, because He first loved us. (1 John 4:19)

> You shall love the LORD your God with all your heart and with all your soul and with all your might. These words, which I am commanding you today, shall be on your heart. You shall teach them diligently to your sons and shall talk of them when you sit in your house and when you walk by the way and when you lie down and when you rise up. You shall bind them as a sign on your hand and they shall be as frontals on your forehead. You shall write them on the doorposts of your house and on your gates. (Deuteronomy 6:5–9)

Jesus affirmed Deuteronomy 6:5 during His ministry on earth, emphasizing our foundational need to return God's love for us. God created us in love and chose to love us; all He desires is for us to love Him back. Reciprocating His love should be the easiest, most natural, most astounding honor and privilege we can pursue. When we begin to realize who He is (which happens incrementally as we study His Word), we begin to understand how unworthy we are even to know about Him, much less communicate and have a relationship with Him. Then, to realize that He not only is even bigger and more fantastic than our feeble minds can comprehend, but actually loves us? That He has made us the objects of His affection? That He desires our good? And then that He orchestrated His Son's gruesome death on a cross so we could be with Him? It is almost literally unbelievable. And all He wants in return is for us to love Him back. This should be the easiest command to obey.

But unfortunately, it's not. Why? Aside from a gross lack of understanding of the gospel, it's because we have such a crude, unsubstantial, erroneous, and sinful understanding of what love is. Genuine love for God requires trust and obedience. God did not wishfully ask us to love Him. He did not write, "I love you. Will you consider loving Me back?" Or, "I'm offering you everything you need and could ever want in Jesus. Will you pretty please love me in return?" It sounds heretical even reading something like that, doesn't it? That's because God does not daintily request our love. He commands it. Following God means loving Him. To love Him is to obey Him. It's to trust that He knows what's best for us and to submit to His leadership and authority.

Consider Jesus's love for the Father, especially when facing the most egregious trial possible:

> And He withdrew from them about a stone's throw, and He knelt down and began to pray, saying, "Father, if You are willing, remove this cup from Me; yet not My will, but Yours be done." (Luke 22:41–42)

> Have this attitude in yourselves which was also in Christ Jesus, who, although He existed in the form of God, did not regard equality with God a thing to be grasped, but emptied Himself, taking the form of a bond-servant, and being made in the likeness of men.

> Being found in appearance as a man, He humbled
> Himself by becoming obedient to the point of death,
> even death on a cross. (Philippians 2:5–8)

Jesus, God-incarnate, exercised His love for the Father through
obedience and trust. He willingly endured the most atrocious,
excruciating death imaginable, all for the sake of love—first for
the Father, and then for humanity. He did not die to accept or
approve of our sin. He died to take the punishment for it.
Genuine love requires utmost selflessness and sacrifice, complete
trust in and obedience to the Father. It demands that we
prioritize Him first at the expense of everything and everyone
else. It means we completely trust who He declares to be in His
Word. We must trust without reserve, not picking and choosing
which areas of our lives we're willing to trust Him with.

It also means being willing to obey, even if we don't understand
or if our obedience requires great personal sacrifice. As He wrote
in Proverbs 3:5–6, "Trust in the Lord with all your heart and do
not lean on your own understanding. In all your ways
acknowledge Him, and He will make your paths straight." Jesus
did exactly that, and while the cross was nearly too much to bear,
His trust and obedience resulted in the salvation of the world.
Jesus loved the Father and loved us more than His personal
comfort.

Because of it, we can spend eternity thanking and being with
Him!

That is yet another beautiful aspect of God's design of love for
humanity. When we love God back as we should, we glorify

Him and accomplish His purposes (the aim of every Christian). Our love for others grows and becomes more automatic as well. The two greatest commandments reflect this design: love God first and wholly, then: "You shall love your neighbor as yourself" (Mark 12:31).

Love for Others

Love is a part of our identity as children of God, but the ways in which it is manifested can change depending on its object. While love for God is executed largely through trust and obedience, our love for others takes on slightly different nuances. (It's not always wise to trust or obey our fellow man. Jesus certainly did not.) As our definition states, to love others is *to seek their (another's) good purposefully, consistently, and sacrificially as defined by God and purposed for His glory.*

Before getting into the nuances of how to love others, we should address one tenet of love that is true regardless of its object: love is not an option. It's not a command to obey only when we feel like it. We love God because He first loved us; we love others because He does, and loving them is how we join His mission on earth.

God is easy to love because He never lets us down. Unfortunately, that's not true with other people. We will always experience disappointment, rejection, broken trust, disloyalty, and other unlovely experiences in our human relationships because we are all fallen creatures. However, that's no excuse to withhold love. Love is not reserved for times when others are loveable. If God loved us only when we were amiable, we'd be objects of His wrath for all eternity. "For all have sinned and fall short of the glory of God" (Romans 3:23). We didn't earn God's love; we don't deserve it, nor could we ever hope to. Our love for others, then, must be the same. It's an extension of God's love toward us, independent of others' attitudes.

As Jesus said in His Sermon on the Mount:

> "You have heard that it was said, 'You shall love your neighbor and hate your enemy.' But I say to you, love your enemies and pray for those who persecute you, so that you may be sons of your Father who is in heaven; for He causes His sun to rise on the evil and the good, and sends rain on the righteous and the unrighteous. For if you love those who love you, what reward do you have? Do not even the tax collectors do the same? If you only greet your brothers, what more are you doing than others? Do not even the Gentiles do the same? Therefore you are to be perfect, as your heavenly Father is perfect." (Matthew 5:43–48)

People in Jesus's day had the same attitude about loving others that most do today—return love for love, hate for hate. To the world, love is a measure of amicability and convenience. It's something people have to earn and continue earning if they want us to continue giving it. If they don't, we think we're off the hook and can move on to someone else. But that's not what Jesus says or did. Jesus says we must not love only our neighbor but also those who actively hate us—who even go so far as persecuting us. That, of course, goes against every fiber of our flesh, which screams either to "fight or flight" those who attack us. But if we're to love like Jesus, we must prioritize people's souls over our ease and see them through the light of eternity rather than our temporary circumstances.

The Bible gives us many verses that show us how to accomplish this, especially regarding our love for one another:

> Love is patient, love is kind and is not jealous; love does not brag and is not arrogant, does not act unbecomingly; it does not seek its own, is not provoked, does not take into account a wrong suffered, does not rejoice in unrighteousness, but rejoices with the truth; bears all things, believes all things, hopes all things, endures all things. Love never fails. (1 Corinthians 13:4–8a)

In this iconic passage, we learn quite a bit about God's design of love and how we are to implement it. This is neither the time nor place for an exhaustive study of this passage. But we'll conduct an aerial-view analysis, paying particular attention to the things these characteristics have in common and how we should manifest them in our lives.

First, as we've seen, love is relational and comes to life only in the context of relationships—first with God, then with others. We must exercise the characteristics of love in our 1 Corinthians 13 passage, but that happens only when we're with others. Head knowledge about each of these aspects of love accomplishes nothing if it doesn't move to our heart (affections) and our hands (actions).

Second, all of these characteristics confirm and advance our definition of love for others: *To love someone is to seek their good purposefully, consistently, and sacrificially as defined by God and purposed for His glory.* Being patient, kind, humble, forgiving, etc. are all purposeful ways we can consistently and sacrificially seek someone else's good for the glory of God.

To illustrate this point, let's briefly consider patience. Jesus was infinitely patient with people. In fact, He never seemed rushed as He conducted His ministry. He was patient with His disciples, constantly explaining things to them that they should've understood (Matthew 16:5–12). He was patient with little children, allowing them to come to Him when society did everything possible to keep them away (Luke 18:16). He was patient with crowds, teaching, listening, and healing for hours upon hours (Luke 9:11–12). He was patient with influential leaders (John 3:1–21), just as he was the poor, sick, and outcast (John 4:7–29; Matthew 4:24; Luke 19:1–8). If anyone had legitimate excuses not to be patient with people, it was God incarnate coming down from heaven to rescue a backslidden, undeserving, thick-skulled people. Yet, Jesus showed utmost patience, purposefully, consistently, and sacrificially seeking their good for God's glory.

Third, loving relationships come in all shapes and sizes. Love is not limited to our relationships with our spouses, children, or other family members. None of the characteristics listed in 1 Corinthians 13 have restrictions that depend on proximity. We're to show patience with our children and with an overwhelmed waitress at a restaurant. At its core, love among mankind is universal. We are not at liberty to be loving toward only those we like. We must exercise godly love to everyone in our lives.

While we must show God's love to everyone, we express varying degrees of love and commitment within our relationships. Let's explore these for a moment—what they look like for us and what they looked like for Jesus. First, let's consider our immediate families. We will obviously, hopefully, and rightfully love our spouses and children more than we do anyone else on earth. Yet this love is not a different entity than the love we show our fellow man; it's merely heightened to more accurately depict and reflect the loving relationships we have with God. Marriage (between one biological and self-identifying man and woman) was designed by God to reflect the relationship between Himself and His people, and between Christ and the church:

> You will also be a crown of beauty in the hand of the LORD, and a royal diadem in the hand of your God. It will no longer be said to you, "Forsaken," nor to your land will it any longer be said, "Desolate"; but you will be called, "My delight is in her," and your land, "Married"; for the Lord delights in you, and to Him your land will be married. For as a young man marries a virgin, so your sons will marry you; and as the bridegroom rejoices over the bride, so your God will rejoice over you. (Isaiah 62:3–5)

> Wives, be subject to your own husbands, as to the Lord. For the husband is the head of the wife, as Christ also is the head of the church, He Himself

being the Savior of the body. But as the church is subject to Christ, so also the wives ought to be to their husbands in everything. Husbands, love your wives, just as Christ also loved the church and gave Himself up for her, so that He might sanctify her, having cleansed her by the washing of water with the word, that He might present to Himself the church in all her glory, having no spot or wrinkle or any such thing; but that she would be holy and blameless....This mystery is great; but I am speaking with reference to Christ and the church. (Ephesians 5:22–27, 32)

These are just two of many examples in which God uses marriage to reflect His relationship with His people. Our spouses (should) know us better than anyone else on earth, and the commitment and unity we share with them directly reflects that of God for us.

However, a heightened capacity to love does not come only with a marriage license. Jesus was not married, yet He loved others better than we could ever hope to. His "bride" is the church—believers who chose to love, trust, and follow Him in the gospel. He is far more loyal, selfless, patient, and kind than we will ever be with our spouses. Jesus displayed God's perfect love for us in every aspect of His life and actions. Thus, while marriage is a beautiful, designated example of the intense and intimate commitment God shows in His love for us, it is certainly not required in order to experience His love on earth.

The parent/child relationship is another beautiful human relationship in which God reveals His love to us. Jesus used this analogy in His teachings (and so did the apostles later on) to help us understand the parent/child relationship we first experience with God:

> Or what man is there among you who, when his son asks for a loaf, will give him a stone? Or if he asks for a fish, he will not give him a snake, will he? If you then, being evil, know how to give good gifts to your children, how much more will your Father who is in heaven give what is good to those who ask Him? (Matthew 7:9–11)

> Therefore you are to be perfect, as your heavenly Father is perfect. (Matthew 5:48)

> Pray, then, in this way: "Our Father who is in heaven…" (Matthew 6:9)

> Now may our Lord Jesus Christ Himself and God our Father, who has loved us and given us eternal comfort… (2 Thessalonians 2:16)

It should not be lost on us that two members of the Trinity are God *the Father* and God *the Son*. This relational description is for our sake, so we can better understand love. Love should be most intimately experienced with God first, and our immediate family (either by blood or by choice) next. These are the closest relationships we have, so they reveal the depths of God's love for us and how we should reciprocate that love to Him.

Our immediate families are usually those who receive the highest concentration of our love. However and interestingly, those in Jesus's inner circle were not biological family members at all. Instead, He instead chose Peter, James, and John.

> And His mother and brothers came to Him, and they were unable to get to Him because of the crowd. And it was reported to Him, "Your mother and Your brothers are standing outside, wishing to see You." But He answered and said to them, "My mother and My brothers are these who hear the word of God and do it."[16]

We must once again reiterate the point that marriage and children are wonderful gifts from the Lord, designed to help us better understand and live out love to bring God glory. However, they are not the only way we can bring God glory through love, nor are they perfect institutions. If you are single, take heart. You are not incomplete, and you're not missing out on some vital, secret aspect of love. While the intimacy of a marital relationship may not be your experience, you can still experience intimacy with Christ. His love is full, unwavering, and satisfying in ways no spouse could ever fulfill.

Remember, Jesus was single. Instead of leaving His family and taking a wife, Jesus "left" His biological family and took up the call of His heavenly Father. Jesus's priority was God's kingdom over the world's. Blood and marriage did not matter nearly as much as aligning Himself with those He predestined to proclaim the gospel after His ascension.

Likewise, those closest to us should be deliberate choices rather than merely default relationships. Even those in closest proximity to us should continually be chosen as objects of our love. We must be intentional about those we love in order to love them to the degree God calls us to in the gospel.[17] Choosing to align ourselves with and love others who are intent on advancing the gospel is prudent, wise, and glorifying to God. Thus, spouse and children relationships are obvious choices when communicating the intimacy and potency of God's love for us. So are friends, mentors, and mentees we choose to invest in. The nature of these relationships doesn't matter nearly as much as the One both are striving after. We get the best glimpses of love possible when we engage in relationships as He designed, prescribed, and exemplified for us in His Word. Regardless of who comprises our "inner circles," we are to use our most intimate relationships to exercise godly love for the purpose of glorifying God.

While those closest to us receive the largest investment of our love, we are still called to maintain a posture of love toward everyone in our lives. From our next-door neighbor to the clerk at the grocery store, God calls us to love everyone, just as Christ did. This kind of love is not manifested in extended time or intense devotion but with a 1 Corinthians 13 demeanor that leaves Jesus's fingerprints on everyone we interact with.

The most helpful way I've found to love others outside my inner circle is to view them in light of eternity. When we see people first and foremost as image-bearers of God, whom He loves and sent His Son to die for, we can't help but love them. When we think about spending eternity with them, it shapes our perspective, posture, and actions in the here and now. It doesn't require much to show His love—a genuine smile and greeting, asking how we can pray for them (and actually doing it), being a good customer, showing respect, offering a compliment, etc. We can easily become the bright spot in someone's day simply by taking time to see them as one of God's unique creations rather than an object or mere bystander.

God gives us both special and general relationships so we can communicate and display truths of His love. This brings us back to our observations about biblical love in 1 Corinthians We've seen how love is relational, how it advances our definition of love, and how those relationships come in various shapes and sizes. Closing this section, I'd like to reiterate how love is a choice. It's a decision we make day in and day out, and so are its characteristics, which we listed in this Corinthian passage. Just as God chose to love us and continually chooses to do so, we must choose to love others and continually live out that choice.

Jesus is the perfect example of every attribute of love mentioned in this passage: "Love is patient, love is kind and is not jealous, love does not brag and is not arrogant, does not act unbecomingly; it does not seek its own, is not provoked, does not take into account a wrong suffered, does not rejoice in unrighteousness, but rejoices with the truth; bears all things, believes all things, hopes all things, endures all things. Love never fails" (1 Corinthians 13:4–8a). Every one of these is a choice He made. We must also make them intentionally and consistently as we go about our lives and invest in our relationships.

Love, then, as noted in the opening of this chapter, is not first a feeling or emotion. It is a decision that may lead to heightened feelings of emotion, but it also may not. Some people are (and may always be) difficult to love. As He was dying on the cross, Jesus cried, "Father, forgive them; for they do not know what they are doing" (Luke 23:34). He loved those who were literally murdering Him and who would naturally be the most difficult of all to love. We may never experience positive emotions toward difficult people. However, nowhere does God say we have to *feel* positively toward someone in order to love them. "We love, because He first loved us."[18] Choosing to love others, even and especially when they are unlovely, is one way we both represent God and reciprocate His love for us.

Love and Truth

Finally, love reflects God and His Word. This point is summed up well with Paul's declaration that love "does not rejoice in unrighteousness, but rejoices with the truth," and later, "Let love be without hypocrisy. Abhor what is evil; cling to what is good" (Romans 12:9). God is righteous; He is truth.

Jesus declared, "I am the way, and the truth, and the life; no one comes to the Father but through Me" (John 14:6). He is righteousness embodied; truth incarnate. Thus, if we are to love others with a godly, righteous love, we must do so synchronized with and exhorting the truth of God's Word.

This stands directly opposed to the world's (ahem, Satan's) definition of love. The world denies truth at worst and deforms it at best. They have no problem loving others if it means encouraging everyone to do whatever makes them feel good. (With the exception of Christians, though. The world doesn't tolerate those of us who believe in absolute truth.) If a man wants to be a woman, the world says go for it. If a woman wants to love another woman, then awesome. If someone wants more than one spouse, the more the merrier! If you never want to get married at all, sleep with countless people of all gender orientations, pop abortion pills like candy, or mutilate children's bodies to help them discover their "true identity," cool. You do you. These stances (and countless more) directly defy God's Word and the order He created and prescribed for humanity. Rejecting the sacred truth of Scripture is not just accepted in the world. It's celebrated.

Liberal theological stances run the risk of making the situation even worse. At times, they blatantly defy God's Word. But it's often more subtle, like Satan with Eve. Since they want to appease the world and not be condemned as narrow-minded and inclusive, they use the Bible to promote their anti-Scripture agenda. They pick and choose excerpts from Scripture (while disregarding others completely) to fuel their biases and make the world like and approve of them. They warp definitions to make themselves (and others) feel better about their unrighteous, ungodly, unholy behavior. They use the name of Christ to promote agendas that defy what He said and who He was.

Case in point: a governor of California once endorsed an ad that read:

Need an abortion? California is ready to help. Learn more at abortion.ca.gov. "Love your neighbor as yourself. There is no greater commandment than these." Mark 12:31 Paid for by Newsom for California Governor 2022

Understandably, Newsom got a lot of backlash for this ad. Apparently, Newsom believes one's "neighbor" is a woman who wants to kill her child, and "loving her" means to provide ways for her to do so. Yet to anyone even remotely familiar with the Bible, "love your neighbor" does not mean empowering women to kill their innocent children. Quite the opposite, actually. Loving our neighbor means empowering them with the truth that life begins at conception and has intrinsic worth as someone created in the image of God. Loving our neighbor also means loving *all* our neighbors, including the ones who aren't yet born.

Divorcing truth from love renders love meaningless. As Paul writes in our 1 Corinthians passage, love "rejoices with the truth" (13:6). We cannot separate love from truth and have even the smallest chance of experiencing it fully. Yet we do it all the time. Both conservatives and liberals are guilty of sacrificing truth on the altar of love; thereby "freeing" ourselves to engage in sinful relationships and activities in our pursuit of it. Look, if sin wasn't fun, no one would do it. It's exciting to give in to temptations and easy to go along with what everyone else is doing.

We're all guilty of divorcing truth from love. The difference is, Christian conservatives know better and will (hopefully) be convicted of our actions, repent, and once again submit to the truth of God's Word. It's the hard road, to be sure, but we realize that disobeying God not only dishonors Him, but it hurts us deeply as well. We cannot separate love from truth because God doesn't and can't. He is both love and truth. Thus, in order to love someone wholly and as God designed it, we must do so as defined by God and purposed for His glory.

Liberal ideology, contrarily, claims truth is relative, or that it doesn't exist at all. They think truth is too restricting, so they rejoice in love and love alone, however they want to define it. Satan is the master of this—he rejoices in *un*righteousness and *slanders* truth. He inspires people to detach love from truth. He wants us to believe that loving others means approving of their personal choices, even (and especially) when it means defying God's Word.

Cheap Love

While much more could be written about biblical love, we will conclude with one more thought: love that is not grounded in and committed to exemplifying truth as defined by Scripture is ultimately cheap. Worldly love apart from the Jesus of Scripture is inferior, deformed, feeble, and deficient. It lacks the strong foundation it needs, both to survive and to thrive as God intended.

As an example, consider the parent of a wayward child. This parent—we will call him Tom—has a daughter, Samantha, whom he loves. He wants what's best for her. Unfortunately,

Tom does not exercise his love for Samantha in ways that honor God and are committed to truth. Because his ultimate goal is her happiness and peace in their father/daughter relationship, Tom lets Samantha do whatever she wants. It starts small. Instead of correcting her when she throws a temper tantrum, he caves to her every whim, rationalizing that her happiness is more important than teaching her a lesson. As she grows, he does not establish or enforce rules about homework or respect. This pattern continues through her teenage years as he bows his will to her flimsy, immature desires and allows her to make her own choices—sleeping around, drugs, drinking, dressing immodestly, no curfew, and not having to work or maintain grades. He refuses to discipline her and accepts all her choices because, he thinks, they are hers to make. All the while, he grasps a faint hope that a switch would magically flip one day and somehow turn her into a respectable woman. Not so surprisingly, that doesn't happen. One day, Tom receives the worst call of his life—his daughter passed away from an accident caused by her drunk driving.

Did Tom love his daughter well? Liberals and those who uphold a worldly perspective would answer yes. He embraced her decisions and let her live as she wanted. He protected her "rights" to make decisions as she pleased—to do what she felt was right and what she believed would make her happy.

Yet Christians would argue that Tom did not love his daughter well at all. In fact, he set her up for failure by not introducing her to (and subsequently enforcing) truth and behaviors that align with God's Word. He did not give her a chance to know God and be transformed by Him; he just hoped she would one day wake up and realize the error of her ways. His commitment to her temporary happiness robbed her of eternal joy and peace. He loved her poorly and cheaply, choosing the easy way out instead of investing in her spiritual, emotional, and even physical well-being. Instead of speaking truth to her in love, he allowed her to believe the ever-shifting lies of this world, and it ultimately led to her demise and his shattered heart.

This, of course, is just one example, and an obviously negative one at that. But what about secular couples who are committed to each other and do well? What about gay couples whose marriages last longer than their Christian counterparts'—who are an "inspiration" to others in their dedication and support of one another? Is their love cheap?

Again, in order to determine the success of a loving relationship, we must define it as Scripture does. Have Bill and Luke (a fictional gay couple for our purposes here) displayed commitment to each other in the thirty years they've been married? Absolutely. And that's most certainly a part of the biblical definition of love. (Remember God's fierce commitment to Israel, and to us, for that matter.) Are Bill and Luke patient, kind, not jealous, not arrogant, not begrudging, and selfless with one another—all characteristics of love as defined by God through the Apostle Paul's words in 1 Corinthians 13? Yes. They exude a wonderful, loving relationship as defined by all those qualifications. To the world, Bill and Luke have a successful, satisfying marriage.

But how does God define their marriage? The answer is clear in Scripture: their marriage is ultimately a failure, if one concedes to its authenticity at all. First, it fails because it rejects God's created and prescribed marital design between one (biological and self-identifying) man and woman. Design and function go hand in hand. You cannot replace a Harley Davidson's wheels with a child's bicycle wheels and think you're honoring the Harley Davidson brand. Such an action would both insult Harley Davidson and ultimately not work at all. Child's bicycle wheels were simply not designed to bear the weight of a Harley—the design of both the child's bike and the Harley would be irreconcilably compromised. The same is true with marriage as designed by God. Any mutation of the design cheapens it. This dishonors God and is reason enough to avoid it. Ultimately, this distortion also won't work as well and won't result in the sanctification of either individual.

While gay marriages and other relationships that defy God's Word may seem to work just fine on earth, they cannot bring Him glory or result in greater faith of either individual. *One cannot develop, mature, and strengthen his/her faith in God while purposefully and defiantly living in sin, contrary to His Word.* It's like expecting Harley to honor a warranty on parts we replace with children's toys. It's not going to work, and it doesn't make sense. When we cheapen or outright destroy the integrity of a product, we can no longer identify it as the original product. Same with marriage and any other loving relationship. Thus, any temporary benefits of such relationships are exactly that—temporary. They are of no benefit to the individual, the church, or the kingdom of God until or unless He redeems it through repentant hearts and godly living as mandated in His Word.

Part of what makes this so hard to swallow is that the world *can* experience love—in part. It's not as though Christians are the only ones who experience love to any kind of meaningful degree. All humans are capable of love, because we're all image-bearers of God. However, we can experience love with eternal significance, spiritual sanctification, and glorification to God only when we love within the parameters He set forth in His Word. His love cannot be separated from His truth. Therefore, in order to love as Christ did, we must uphold truth as we strive to glorify God by selflessly seeking the good—and sanctification—of others.

God's love for us is not cheap, and it certainly was not easy. It was not the fun, satisfying, go-with-the-crowd kind of love. In fact, it cost Him more than any of us could ever imagine enduring:

> For God so loved the world, that He gave His only begotten Son, that whoever believes in Him shall not perish, but have eternal life. (John 3:16)

This verse is probably the most popular verse in Scripture, which is great. But familiarity can breed apathy. Think about the message here, particularly regarding what loving us cost God—*He gave His only begotten Son*. Parents, can you imagine purposefully sending your child to his/her death? There's no way. Not even for a righteous cause would I send one of our daughters to die. Nope, nope, nope. Every fiber in a parent's being seeks to protect their children from harm at all cost. We would absolutely give our lives to protect them. But send them to their death? Absolutely not. I can think of no greater pain than losing a child. I cannot comprehend giving one up to death for the sake of loving someone else.

That is the expense of God's love for us, made even worse by the fact that He did it for people who despised, mocked, disobeyed, rejected, and defiled His name. He did not sacrificially give His Son to a people who reciprocated His love. It would have been one thing if we recognized our depravity and relentlessly begged for God to save us. If we had humbled ourselves in obedience, doing everything within our power to pursue righteousness, justice, and holiness, then maybe, just maybe, that would have made it a little easier for Him. The cost would still be astronomical, but at least being appreciated would have taken a bit of the sting out of the sacrifice.

But no.

Jesus willingly went to the cross for people who hated Him. He suffered and gave His life for a world who overwhelmingly rejected Him, His truth, and His love. The cross was the most expensive and painful expression of love the world could ever fathom, much less experience. And He did it while knowing that the majority of this world would continue to reject, defame, and make a mockery of both Him and His love.

That's one reason the deforming of truth and God's created order is such a gross offense to the Lord. He gave everything to show His love and offer us a way to love Him back and be with Him. And some self-professing Christians cannot even manage to acquiesce His most basic and fundamental design for us. We can't burden ourselves with loving Him back in the manner He literally died in order to make possible. Can we not pay the comparatively miniscule, trivial price of abiding by His Word?

We cheapen God's love and rob it of its power when we fail to live by the truth it's founded upon. When we disregard His Word, we settle for a cheap imitation of love rather than the genuine, costly, eternal product. We outfit a Harley with children's tires, tinsel, and a lopsided pink basket and deceive ourselves into thinking it's the same thing—or worse, that it's an improved version. We can't experience genuine, God-centered love apart from Him, and it's high time we stop trying. We need to trust in and abide by the One who is love. We need to stop choosing selfish, worldly pursuits and usurping His authority and will for our lives. And we need to follow Jesus's example in the Scriptures instead of distorting it to accommodate lies and secular preferences that blatantly contradict His very nature and written Word.

Chapter Six
Suffering

Myth:

Jesus sought only good for others, and He wants only the best for us. He suffered so we won't have to, and if we have enough faith and do enough good works, we won't.

Truth Within the Myth:

Jesus does seek our good and does not take pleasure in our suffering.

Where Truth Gets Distorted by a Lie:

As we've seen, Satan wants to thwart the gospel however he can. He hates God, despises humanity, and wants everyone to join him forever in his miserable existence. He uses many tactics to accomplish his evil purposes, including confusing language and getting others to doubt and question God. Now we'll tackle another of his tactics: suffering. Sometimes he uses suffering to try to make people turn away from God (as he did with Job). At other times, he uses the threat of suffering to keep people complacent and unwilling to voice truth. Regardless of the tactic, his motivation is always the same: get as many people as far from God as possible.

Unfortunately, he succeeds quite often. That's why it's imperative that we, as Christians, understand truth and have a healthy theological framework to shape our worldview. We cannot fight back if we don't have the proper weapons and know how to use them. Imagine a grown man picking a fight with a ten-year-old boy. The child doesn't stand a chance unless someone had adequately prepared him for the situation and had given him the proper training and tools to fight back. When it comes to Satan, we are at a significant disadvantage. We're not nearly as smart, cunning, or powerful as he is. However, we serve the smartest, most powerful God. We simply need to learn to use the power of the Holy Spirit to fight back.

We need to acknowledge and embrace two main truths about suffering: first, it's inevitable, and second, it can be a powerful tool of sanctification.

Since suffering is a huge topic, we'll start with a big-picture perspective and then move toward a narrower focus, starting with the origin of suffering and then moving to types of suffering, responses to suffering, the purpose of suffering, and finally Jesus and suffering. This will help us to think through truth so we can embrace and then use that truth to draw us closer to God (thereby conquering Satan) when suffering presents itself.

The Origin of Suffering

To develop a proper biblical understanding of suffering, we need to go back to Genesis 3. We already analyzed the way Satan distorted God's words to Adam and Eve in a way that led to sin entering the world. Yet one often-overlooked consequence of the fall is the introduction to suffering. Prior to the fall, Adam and Eve had no idea what suffering was. While they engaged in work, it was pleasant, fulfilling, and painless. They could work hard without overtiring, accomplish as much as they wanted without resistance, work together in perfect harmony, and rest peacefully without encountering failure or disappointment. But after they sinned, they learned that one of the consequences of their eventual physical death was the immediate death of carefree lives:

> To the woman He said, "I will greatly multiply your pain in childbirth, in pain you will bring forth children; yet your desire will be for your husband, and he will rule over you." Then to Adam He said, "Because you have listened to the voice of your wife, and have eaten from the tree about which I commanded you, saying, 'You shall not eat from it'; cursed is the ground because of you; in toil you will eat of it all the days of your life. Both thorns and thistles it shall grow for you; and you will eat the plants of the field; by the sweat of your face you will eat bread, till you return to the ground, because from it you were taken; for you are dust, and to dust you shall return." (Genesis 3:16–19)

Eve's introduction to suffering would be physical, and it would be a doozy—greatly increased pain in childbirth. As someone who has delivered four babies (three without medication), let me tell you this would be a shocking and excruciating way to encounter serious suffering for the first time. They don't call it the "ring of fire" for nothing. And since one of Eve's primary responsibilities was to "be fruitful and multiply," she had to endure this pain a lot.

But Eve's suffering wouldn't be limited to physical pain. It would also be relational. Until the fall, she and Adam had a perfect marriage. Communication was great, sex was fantastic—they were both fulfilled completely in both their relationship with God and with each other. But once sin entered the world, friction entered their marriage. What was once effortless became difficult; what had always been a joy was now littered with resentment, misunderstandings, and frustration.

Adam's introduction to suffering was also physical and relational, though in different ways. First, he suffered physically because he would have to exert much more effort in harvesting food than he ever had before. No longer would the ground produce food flawlessly—watered perfectly by dew, nurtured by uncorrupted soil, free of thorns and thistles. Now his work would be laborious. While he'd undoubtedly still find fulfillment in it, it would also be backbreaking, deflating, and agonizing. He'd sweat, get blisters, injure muscles, and get frustrated when things went wrong.

The suffering in his work would be exacerbated by the reason he was pursuing it in the first place: his position to provide and care for his ever-increasing family. If he did not work, they literally did not eat. They were kicked out of the garden that provided food for them effortlessly. Now they had to work to eat, and the number of mouths to feed increased every year. Thus, in addition to the physical hardships they incurred, Adam experienced pressure both emotionally and relationally. A lot of people depended on him, and he would forever struggle in his efforts, which were likely made even worse by his memories of how good he had it before the fall.

As seen in Adam's curse, nature itself would suffer from sin as well. Before the fall, there were no weeds, thorns, or thistles. There was no bad weather and no setbacks in farming or harvesting. Everything the earth produced was bountiful, substantial, delicious, and easy to procure. All that changed with the fall, though, both on earth and in the animal kingdom. Adam named the animals before the fall and maintained a harmonious relationship with them. After the fall, distrust and fear replaced confidence and peace. No longer did mankind and the animal kingdom live in harmony, nor did the animal kingdom live harmoniously within itself.

Suffering entered the world with sin, and nothing escaped its destructive grip. It became the new reality—the expectation of life in a fallen world. Adam and Eve had to adjust to it; we as their descendants have been born into it and can't avoid it. The main point to note here is that the origin of suffering lies with man and his choice to sin despite God's warnings and promises of abundant life. God didn't cause sin, but He did allow it when He gave them free choice.

Types of Suffering

Just as suffering impacted the world in various degrees after the fall, so it continues to manifest itself in numerous forms today. One of the most obvious forms of suffering is physical, including sickness, disease, and brokenness in our bodies. Physical suffering is common, though on a vastly diverse scale. These infirmities range from annoying to excruciating, and from temporary to long-term. No one is immune to the physical suffering of sickness and disease; even the most health-conscience individual can't escape at least some form of sickness.

Another aspect of physical suffering, at least in regard to tangibility, is that of finances and poverty. While most of us have everything we need (properly distinguishing between needs and wants is a subject for another book), we do not have everything we want. We often perceive that lack as suffering. Having a $20,000 car instead of an $80,000 one is not suffering. Neither is wearing clothes from second-hand stores instead of new name-brand ones. Examples are endless. Americans also tend to whine vastly disproportionally to any actual suffering.

Some, however, genuinely do not have their basic needs met (food, clothing, and shelter). Their financial suffering is real and inevitably leads to other forms of physical suffering, including illness and malnourishment. Physical suffering encompasses a host of infirmities, bodily and otherwise. All are either directly or indirectly the result of sin.

Also unavoidable is relational suffering. Because we are all sinful people, there is no escaping hurt, anger, disappointment, and other measures of suffering in relationships. Some suffering, of course, is worse than others. At one extreme, individuals are victims of horrendous abuse at the hands of their spouses or guardians. One in four women have experienced physical violence from an intimate partner,[19] and ninety-five percent of men who are physically abusive to their partners are also emotionally abusive to them.[20] Another form of relational suffering is sexual. It is estimated that one American is sexually assaulted every seventy-three seconds, including around 60,000 children per year.[21] Child abuse in other forms is rampant too—a report of child abuse is made every ten seconds in the United States.[22] Suffering at the hands of those who are supposed to love, nurture, and protect us is despicable and a gross deformity of the created order God established for us in the beginning.

Yet suffering exists in less-dramatic relational forms as well. Misunderstandings, anger, disappointment, and general conflict are forms of suffering that take a significant toll on people. I had a college friend who had unsupportive, critical parents. Nothing she did pleased them. They subtly criticized or blatantly mocked every one of her pursuits. This led to serious issues with her identity and confidence. She struggled daily to view herself in light of God's Word when all she heard in her mind were the rejections her parents had spewed upon her over the years. This kind of suffering is never reported because it's not considered "that bad" (and she certainly was never at any risk of physical harm). But she's had to fight her whole life to believe truth *in spite* of her upbringing, whereas God wants us to know and love Him more *because* of our upbringing.

Relational suffering is potent and sometimes inescapable, as is another form of suffering: emotional. Emotional abuse in relationships is inexcusable and a disgusting perversion of God's created order. Yet we endure the much more subtle emotional suffering every day, because our emotions are broken, fallible, and unreliable. We battle with them constantly if we're living for the Lord. Emotions are not inherently bad. God has emotions and gifted us with them as well. Life would be boring without emotions—without butterflies in your stomach when you see your beloved, without the weightless thrill you experience when you get a promotion or your child experiences a victory, or without laughter and humor shared with friends over dinner. Emotions are wonderful, but they're also victims of suffering because of sin.

Instead of accurately reflecting and supporting truth, we often impulsively and unwisely follow our emotions when our circumstances change. For instance, what happens when our child throws a football in the house (again!) when he knows he's not supposed to, and he breaks the heirloom vase passed down in our family for generations? We get angry, snap, and let our emotions take over. We give in to anger and justify our actions that come from it. While it's okay to be angry (Jesus got angry), it's never okay to sin in our anger or any other emotion. When we let emotions dictate our decisions, the result will usually be sin. What's worse, the more we follow our emotions, the further we move from God and His Word. Instead of growing in our sanctification and becoming more like Him, we shrivel in our sin and become more like the devil.

Emotions are powerful, but they struggle immensely from the sin that contaminates our minds, hearts, bodies, and souls. We need to recognize their power and our tendencies to succumb to them, then combat and control them with the truth of God's Word.

Physical, relational, and emotional suffering are each distinct, yet not removed from the spiritual suffering that plagues us all. Even the most pious, dedicated, righteous person experiences deep conflict between flesh and spirit. The Apostle Paul did:

> For we know that the Law is spiritual, but I am of flesh, sold into bondage to sin. For what I am doing, I do not understand; for I am not practicing what I would like to do, but I am doing the very thing I hate. But if I do the very thing I do not want to do, I agree with the Law, confessing that the Law is good. So now, no longer am I the one doing it, but sin which dwells in me. For I know that nothing good dwells in me, that is, in my flesh; for the willing is present in me, but the doing of the good is not. For the good that I want, I do not do, but I practice the very evil that I do not want...I see a different law in the members of my body, waging war against the law of my mind and making me a prisoner of the law of sin which is in my members. (Romans 7:14–19, 23)

Sin has comprehensively tainted us and will continue doing so as long as we live on earth. Even though the Holy Spirit does miraculous work, transforming us into the image of

Christ when we embrace and believe the gospel, we are never totally free from sin. Our spirits always struggle, so we will always experience some degree of suffering as we wrestle with the sin that wants to entangle us, paralyze us, and render us useless in the kingdom of God.

A final type of suffering worth noting is that which occurs in nature. We read about this briefly in the creation account. But things have only gotten worse, and creation itself longs for the restoration that will come to fruition one day in Christ:

> For the anxious longing of the creation waits eagerly for the revealing of the sons of God. For the creation was subjected to futility, not willingly, but because of Him who subjected it, in hope that the creation itself also will be set free from its slavery to corruption into the freedom of the glory of the children of God. For we know that the whole creation groans and suffers the pains of childbirth together until now. (Romans 8:19–22)

Suffering is quite apparent in nature. Every year we seem to have at least one natural disaster or catastrophe, ranging from tornadoes to famines, even global pandemics. The world is constantly bombarded with the effects of sin, even though nature itself did nothing to contribute to it in the first place. It was a beautiful, innocent, impartial bystander corrupted by the choices of man and still is today.

As we've seen, suffering is multi-faceted and experienced in numerous ways: physically, relationally, emotionally, spiritually, and in nature. Unfortunately, we are plagued by each of these to varying degrees every day of our lives. Suffering began in Eden but is perpetuated by us and the sin we bring into the world. Since suffering will never be fully eradicated this side of heaven, we Christians do our best to cope with it. Sometimes we cope well. Other times, not so much. But we need to understand common coping mechanisms in order to make the best, most God-honoring decisions.

Responses to Suffering

Suffering happens both to us and because of us. Certain aspects of suffering are well within our control, while others remain outside it. Suffering at the hand of natural disasters, for example, is something we cannot prevent, manipulate, or avoid. We do our best to predict it, but we can only hope for the best and work hard to restore things once disaster has struck. Same with many diseases and sicknesses. Cancer is an impartial predator. It attacks super-healthy gym buffs just as it does the obese couch potato. While certain actions can be taken to help thwart it, complete prevention is impossible.

However, we can control and/or prevent other forms of suffering. Many times, by the decisions we make, we invite suffering to our homes, prepare a feast for it, and ask it to stay a while. For example, finances. Some financial woes happen to us—the stock market crashes, we lose our job unexpectedly, our car breaks down, a loved one falls ill, etc. But many are the result of our own doing. My dad is a financial advisor and has told me horror stories. Some of his clients have passed away and left substantial resources to their child—sometimes insane amounts that could provide comfort and ease for the rest of his/her life if handled responsibly and invested well. Yet that's often not what happened. Typically, when someone without money comes into a substantial sum, he squanders his inheritance faster than a kid can scarf down a doughnut. He'd be penniless (again) in a matter of months, if not weeks. Our own choices cause this kind of suffering, and we have no one to blame but ourselves.

We may or may not be responsible for the suffering that enters our lives, but we absolutely are responsible for our response. We usually respond to it in one of three ways: denial, obsession, or acceptance of the suffering as a tool used for our sanctification.

First, some people choose to deny, avoid, and/or ignore suffering. Consider a woman in an abusive marriage. She loves her husband, so she makes excuse after excuse for him when he hits her. "Oh, he was just upset about something that happened at work," or "He didn't mean to push me that hard. It was an accident," or "Well, it was my fault because I burned dinner." While denial may act as a Band-Aid and make her feel better about what's happening, it's unproductive and harmful.

Another example of denial can be seen regarding our health. For example, one day while shaving, a man notices an abnormal lump in his throat. He thinks it's strange, but he isn't too worried about it, so he carries on, hoping it'll go away. Unfortunately, it doesn't. It continues to grow, and since he can hide it behind his shirt collar, he keeps slaving away at work, meeting deadlines, appeasing clients, and chasing his career goals. Despite knowing the lump is there, and experiencing a few other particular symptoms, he refuses to make time to address it and denies its existence. This kind of denial is unproductive and harmful, because the longer he ignores it, the more dangerous the situation gets.

The bottom line of denial as a response to suffering is that it's temporary, superficial appeasement that allows the real issue to grow exponentially worse. Long-term denial accomplishes nothing but harm. Denying reality will never allow one to escape suffering.

Obsession is another common response to suffering. When something bad happens to someone, he/she cannot stop thinking about and obsessing over it. This prevents true healing from occurring and acts as a poison that seeps into every other aspect of the person's life.

I know a woman who responded to suffering in this way. When she was younger, she was diagnosed with cancer and went through all the brutal treatments and medicines to beat it. Fortunately, she did beat it and has been in remission ever since—nearly two decades now. Yet, every time I talk to her, she brings cancer into the conversation somehow. Every. Single. Time. She's obsessed. Her suffering was absolutely legitimate and horrendously awful, but she continues to suffer because she can't let it go. She experienced physical healing but has yet to find emotional healing or spiritual freedom because she continues fixating on it. Cancer will forever be a miraculous part of the story in which God granted her healing, so she shouldn't pretend it never happened. But by allowing herself to be consumed by it, she refuses to let God redeem it and give her true victory.

Another example of obsession can be found regarding natural disasters. These encounters with suffering are also completely outside our control. Most everyone has experienced some kind of natural disaster, either directly or by having life disrupted in order to avoid it. A specific example ransacked our country and the world not long ago. It wasn't a matter of weather, but rather a matter of health—the worldwide pandemic known as Covid-19. While it was admittedly a terrible ordeal and caused the deaths of millions around the world, the overwhelming majority of cases had positive endings. The survival rate was well over 95 percent, especially for normally healthy individuals. Yet, people were absolutely obsessed with it. Some were terrified and went through extreme measures to avoid contracting it—obsessively washing hands beyond the recommended amount, cleaning around the clock, refusing to socialize, wearing multiple masks at one time, etc. Fear consumed the hearts and minds of so many, and it's incredibly sad. This kind of obsessive paranoia accomplishes nothing, and it paralyzes everyone who possesses it.

Let's briefly look at Paul's words to the Philippian church that shed light on the foolishness of negative obsession:

> Not that I have already attained it or have already become perfect, but I press on so that I may lay hold of that for which also I was laid hold of by Christ Jesus. Brethren, I do not regard myself as having laid

hold of it yet; but one thing I do: *forgetting what lies behind and reaching forward to what lies ahead, I press on toward the goal for the prize of the upward call of God in Christ Jesus.* (Philippians 3:12–14, emphasis added)

Notice Paul's perspective of the past, particularly anything that was a hindrance to his sanctification—"forgetting what lies behind me and reaching forward to what lies ahead…" Paul knew that focusing on the past would only cripple him and hinder his pursuit of Christ. Instead of wallowing in memories of former status or accomplishments (as he is speaking about here), he made the conscious decision to reach forward and press on toward the call God placed on his life. We can say the same of his suffering. God's call on his life made things infinitely more difficult for him, as God told Ananias right before Paul received the Holy Spirit: "He is a chosen instrument of Mine, to bear My name before the Gentiles and kings and the sons of Israel; for I will show him how much he must suffer for My name's sake" (Acts 9:15–16). Paul's entire ministry was marked with suffering, but instead of throwing a pity party, he kept his eyes on Jesus and pushed forward one day at a time.

Obsession with the past (either of past suffering or past successes in light of current suffering), stunts spiritual growth. The only events in the past worth our unwavering, hyperfocused attention are the crucifixion and resurrection of Jesus Christ. That single event is the only instance of suffering we should obsess about, because it alone enables us to persevere in our faith today.

Neither denial nor obsession with suffering accomplishes anything but further harm. They might give some relief, but it's temporary and ultimately a mirage. There is, however, a third and best coping mechanism for suffering: allowing God to use it as a tool for sanctification. We will observe one brief passage to use as an example of this. Here are Paul's words in his letter to the Corinthian church:

> But we have this treasure in earthen vessels, so that the surpassing greatness of the power will be of God and not from ourselves; we are afflicted in every way, but not crushed; perplexed, but not despairing; persecuted, but not forsaken; struck down, but not destroyed; always carrying about in the body the dying of Jesus, so that the life of Jesus also may be manifested in our body. For we who live are constantly being delivered over to death for Jesus' sake, so that the life of Jesus also may be manifested in our mortal flesh...Therefore we do not lose heart, but though our outer man is decaying, yet our inner man is being renewed day by day. For momentary, light affliction is producing for us an eternal weight of glory far beyond all comparison, while we look not at the things which are seen, but at the things which are not seen; for the things which are seen are temporal, but the things which are not seen are eternal. (2 Corinthians 4:7–11,16–18)

We must first note that Paul describes himself and other apostles in full-time ministry. However, we can glean several principles, along with their appropriate application for us, in these passages, particularly in regard to suffering. First, Paul recognizes that he (and other Christians) are but vessels carrying and sharing the treasure of the gospel. This point is crucial for establishing and maintaining not only a proper perspective of suffering, but also the gospel in general. We are not our own. We do not exist for our own purposes; we exist to honor and advance God's. In order to accomplish that, we need to make ourselves ready for God to use us and humbly allow Him to do so as He sees fit, even if that includes suffering. Suffering may not mesh with our agendas, but if it's happening, it meshes with God's agenda for us. And who are we to argue or claim to have a better plan?

> Who are you, O man, who answers back to God? The thing molded will not say to the molder, "Why did you make me like this," will it? Or does the potter have a right over the clay, to make from the same lump one vessel for honorable use and another for common use? What if God, although willing to demonstrate His wrath and to make His power known, endured with much patience vessels of wrath prepared for destruction? And He did so to make known the riches of His glory upon vessels of mercy, which He prepared beforehand for glory. (Romans 9:20–23)

Bottom line? We, as created beings, have no standing, right, or merit to question God, the Creator. He made us exactly as He wanted us and allows us to experience both good and bad, rain and shine, hardship and ease.

Only when we understand, accept, and embrace this truth can we partner with God in the work of sanctification. Notice what Paul says next in our 2 Corinthians passage: "So that the surpassing greatness of the power will be of God and not from ourselves." Yielding ourselves to God allows His power to pour in and through us. Let's use the vessel analogy again. If we, as vessels, are full to the brim with our own agendas, misaligned perspectives, ignorance, etc., there is little to no room left for God and His power to fill us. Now, God can and sometimes does make room, whether we willingly give it to Him or not. But it works oh, so much better when we come to Him with empty vessels and allow Him to fill us however He wants!

One purpose of God's power in our lives is to strengthen us when we face adversity, trials, and suffering. Note Paul's next words: "We are afflicted in every way, but not crushed; perplexed, but not despairing; persecuted, but not forsaken; struck down, but not destroyed." Those of us who are in Christ cannot be defeated by the world, because we already stand victorious over it through the death and resurrection of Jesus.

Paul elaborates on this point in the final verses of our Corinthians passage: "For momentary, light affliction is producing for us an eternal weight of glory far beyond all comparison, while we look not at the things which are seen, but at the things which are not seen; for the things which are seen are temporal, but the things which are not seen are eternal." Our suffering and affliction is real, but in comparison to the eternal damnation we deserve but have been saved from, it is, indeed, light. Even the most gruesome struggles of physical pain or abuse are but a pinprick compared to the agony those without Christ will experience for eternity.

Likewise, our suffering is temporary. In the pit of suffering, it's difficult to see anything clearly, much less believe the pain will ever end. But in Christ, we are assured that everything on earth is temporary and fading away. Paul encourages Christians to keep the gospel perspective when enduring trials and tribulations. He instructs us to look at the things which are not seen, because those are eternal. The gospel is sacred, and it cannot be impacted, sidetracked, derailed, or interrupted by any circumstance in this world. God is establishing His kingdom on a cosmic scale, and the powers of hell will not prevail against Him.

Knowing Who we belong to and the eternal trajectory of our lives gives us every ounce of power needed to endure any suffering the world throws our way. Only when we understand, embrace, and persevere in this perspective will we partner with the Holy Spirit in our sanctification and receive the power we need to endure even the most daunting suffering in this world. We do not need to use futile coping mechanisms like denial or obsession to deal with suffering when we have the power not only to endure it, but also to stand victorious over it.

We need to address one final response to suffering: the dangerous "prosperity gospel" being preached today. I believe Satan uses the men and women who preach this "gospel," harming the kingdom of God they think they arduously advocate.

Televangelists make ridiculous sums of money preaching a prosperity gospel—that if we have enough faith, tithe enough, and abide by the rules, God will ensure our prosperity without suffering. Pain and misery, they claim, are simply the result of failing to live by faith. They use the following verses (taken grossly out of context) to advocate their positions:

> God causes all things to work together for good to those who love God, to those who are called according to His purpose. (Romans 8:28)

> "Ask, and it will be given to you; seek, and you will find; knock, and it will be opened to you. For everyone who asks receives, and he who seeks finds, and to him who knocks it will be opened." (Matthew 7:7–8)

> "'For I know the plans that I have for you,' declares the Lord, '"plans for welfare and not for calamity to give you a future and a hope."' (Jeremiah 29:11)

> You ask and do not receive, because you ask with wrong motives, so that you may spend it on your pleasures. (James 4:3)

> "I came that they may have life, and have it abundantly." (John 10:10b)

> Beloved, I pray that in all respects you may prosper and be in good health, just as your soul prospers. (3 John 1:2)

At first glance, these verses do, indeed, seem to indicate God wants us to prosper on earth—to have health, wealth, and happiness. But like every other myth in this book, such conclusions are based on a superficial, shallow, and deformed understanding of God and His Word. While overtly theatrical messages spewing forth from corny televangelists may be easy to see through, the average Christian may buy into this message more than he/she initially thinks. At the core of this faulty theology (or perhaps another side of the same coin) is works-based salvation and sanctification—believing we can earn salvation and/or keep it through our good works and deeds. Most of us struggle with this because it's exceedingly difficult to believe we really do nothing to earn our salvation, that we play no part in attaining it for ourselves. To believe salvation is completely God's grace, based not at all on us, runs contrary to every bone in our worldly bodies. Yet that is salvation; that is the gospel.

Many people grasp the truth that salvation is initially a gift from God and not of ourselves, yet fall back into a works-based theology in an attempt to *keep* our salvation and/or accomplish our own sanctification. The Apostle Paul recognized this tendency in the Galatian church:

Are you so foolish? Having begun by the Spirit, are you now being perfected by the flesh? (Galatians 3:3)

Therefore you are no longer a slave, but a son; and if a son, then an heir through God. (Galatians 4:7)

> It was for freedom that Christ set us free; therefore
> keep standing firm and do not be subject again to a
> yoke of slavery. (Galatians 5:1)

The Galatians were not living out the freedom they had in the gospel. Instead, they had succumbed to a works-based theology, far more concerned about the Law than God's grace.

What does this have to do with the prosperity gospel? Works and control. The prosperity gospel wants all our attention and focus on what we do and get, specifically what we can do in order to get good standing and/or favor with God. If we can earn our salvation and/or further merit from God, then we can manipulate Him into doing what we want. We then have a God we can control—a God who serves us, not One we serve.

If we can earn our salvation and a good, easy life, suffering becomes easy to explain and fix. If we suffer, it's because we're not doing enough. Do more, do better, and our suffering will cease. The prosperity gospel advocates that God wants our success and leaves it up to us to embrace it or not. The weight of success, salvation, sanctification, and happiness, therefore, rests on our shoulders.

While parts of this theory are appealing, especially to our control-hungry, worldly selves, it's ultimately a complete distortion of reality and a blatant misrepresentation of Jesus and Scripture. Once again, we need to study Scripture in context in order to establish correct theology and see through the lies Satan tells to poison the church. Suffering is an intrinsic part of life on earth, and while God does not take pleasure in our suffering, He does use it for a greater purpose.

The Purpose of Suffering

We have now reviewed the origin and types of suffering, along with common responses. But all that will bear no fruit unless we also understand suffering's purpose. While God did not cause suffering, He can and does use it for two purposes: for our good and His glory. We will briefly explore both of these purposes.

First, how can God use suffering for our good? How is it ever good to suffer? In a culture addicted to comfort, ease, and convenience, suffering is nearly a curse word. The American *pursuit* of happiness has transformed into an *expectation* of happiness. We believe happiness and ease are inherent rights, so we think we're justified in being upset and acting out when our happiness is compromised. We believe we shouldn't have to accommodate or endure suffering. If it does befall us, we do everything possible to ignore or get past it, or it paralyzes us and/or consumes every part of our lives.

Such a worldview of suffering is treacherously unbiblical. Again, suffering is the result of sin, and as long as a bunch of sinners live in a sin-infested world, we'll inevitably suffer. It's inescapable, yet it plays a distinct role in the gospel. Someone said we contribute nothing to the gospel except the reason it's needed in the first place. The fact is, we wouldn't need the good news of Christ if we hadn't so completely and irreversibly screwed things up in the first place. But since we did, and since sin and consequential suffering will always be a reality for us, we desperately need a Savior. We desperately need Jesus.

One crucial purpose of suffering, then, is to point us to Christ. Those with lives of relative ease and comfort—those who don't currently suffer and aren't aware of suffering around them—are much less likely to come to (or grow in) faith because they don't easily recognize their need for Jesus. Consider the rich ruler who approached Jesus:

> A ruler questioned Him, saying, "Good Teacher, what shall I do to inherit eternal life?" And Jesus said to him, "Why do you call Me good? No one is good except God alone. You know the commandments, 'Do not commit adultery, do not murder, do not steal, do not bear false witness, honor your father and mother.'" And he said, "All these things I have kept from my youth." When Jesus heard this, He said to him, "One thing you still lack; sell all that you possess and distribute it to the poor, and you shall have treasure in heaven; and come, follow Me." But when he had heard these things, he became very sad, for he was extremely rich. And Jesus looked at him and said, "How hard it is for those who are wealthy to enter the kingdom of God! For it is easier for a camel to go through the eye of a needle than for a rich man to enter the kingdom of God." (Luke 18:18–25)

This man had everything the world could offer—great wealth, status, presumably good health. The only thing he wanted to add to his portfolio was assurance that he would inherit eternal life. Jesus told him to keep the commandments, which he said he did. Even though no one keeps them perfectly (and Jesus knew this ruler certainly hadn't), Jesus looked through all that and saw the real issue preventing the man from coming to faith—the ruler loved his wealth more than he loved God. He'd likely never known any kind of real suffering, yet that's exactly what Jesus called him to do. It would be excruciating for the ruler to sell everything he had and then give it away to the poor. Such an action would likely be the most painful thing the ruler could endure, for it is what held priority in his heart. Yet Jesus knew that only the surgical removal of misplaced priorities could clear the way for the ruler to enter His kingdom. Jesus extended the ruler an invitation to suffer, at least temporarily, to stop clinging to the world, and to start clinging to God.

Contrarily, the poor, sick, and downtrodden flocked to Jesus and surrounded Him nearly everywhere He went during His ministry on earth. They were acutely aware of their suffering; they experienced a painful longing to be made whole and well. The world had nothing to offer them; in fact, the world had largely rejected them. Recognizing and clinging to Jesus, then, was a no-brainer. Consider the brief account of the poor widow in Mark:

> And He sat down opposite the treasury, and began observing how the people were putting money into the treasury; and many rich people were putting in large sums. A poor widow came and put in two small copper coins, which amount to a cent. Calling His disciples to Him, He said to them, "Truly I say to you, this poor widow put in more than all the contributors to the treasury; for they all put in out of their surplus, but she, out of her poverty, put in all she owned, all she had to live on." (Mark 12:41–44)

This poor widow had nothing, almost literally. Women were not given the same opportunities as they are today—their well-being and financial security depended almost exclusively on their spouses. If a woman's husband died, she was often left with nothing, since the estate and any other wealth typically went to the next male relative, who could choose to provide for her...or not. What Jesus was watching, then, was exactly what He said—she put all she owned into the temple treasury. A woman who endured suffering every day of her life chose to invest in the kingdom over and above her own welfare. She chose to give to the point that she didn't know if she would eat later that day. She chose to invest the very little she had in eternity, not the fleeting things of this world. Did she have to? Absolutely not. Her money was certainly not an encumbrance to her faith. But she did give, and Jesus used it to teach His disciples a valuable lesson.

But perhaps what the text does *not* say and what Jesus did *not* do are most important. Jesus absolutely noticed her suffering, yet we see zero mention of Him alleviating it. He did not give her money. He did not give her a year's supply of food or even a single meal. He didn't transform her two small copper coins into two hundred gold ones. He didn't even praise her to her face. Such a lack of action (especially from Jesus) makes social justice advocates and most liberals cringe. Jesus wasn't concerned about equity or being fair; He didn't provide her with an income to alleviate her financial suffering. He didn't take some of the ruler's wealth and divert it to her. Rather, He honored her faith from afar, noting her wisdom and the intentional sacrifice she made for God. Jesus knew her earthly suffering was producing the best possible result—entrance into the kingdom of God and eternal wealth beyond measure. She would forever bask in the presence of the One she loved most. Her reward would be God, and both she and Jesus knew that nothing else mattered.

The text also does not mention any desire on her part to get rich or end her financial suffering. She didn't cry out to God in pain or for relief, nor did she use her remaining futile funds as a bargaining chip, expecting God to bless her because she gave Him all she had. No. This woman was content, even in her physical suffering. She did not care about her physical or financial status, because it paled in comparison to her relationship with God. Her heart was pure, her relationship with God was secure, and her focus was on God and what she had in Him. She didn't focus on what she did *not* have in the world; she didn't care about that at all. The world may have thought she suffered. But she knew what the world didn't then and doesn't today: true suffering is being separated from God, and no amount of physical wealth, status, or security can touch what God makes available to us in Christ.

Both of these examples show how God uses suffering for our good. The trick, of course, is to define "good" as He does, to keep His Word in context and align our perspective with His. He is far more interested in our *eternal* security and prosperity than He is in our temporary, earthly pleasure. In fact, He knows that, as with the rich young ruler, worldly comfort and success often detract people from faith and reliance on Him. Jesus made it very clear:

> "If anyone wishes to come after Me, he must deny himself, and take up his cross and follow Me. For

whoever wishes to save his life will lose it; but whoever loses his life for My sake will find it. For what will it profit a man if he gains the whole world and forfeits his soul? Or what will a man give in exchange for his soul?" (Matthew 16:24–26)

The rich ruler valued his comfort more than salvation. He was blind to his need for God because his earthly needs were taken care of quite well. Little did he realize that suffering was only way he'd gain riches that mattered. He had the whole world but forfeited his soul because he couldn't take up the cross of self-denial.

How often do we do the same?

We avoid suffering like a plague because we define "good" as comfort, ease, security, and happiness. But God invites us to enter suffering, not for the sake of misery, but to purposefully detach ourselves from the lusts of this world so we can turn our focus to Him. As long as we're chasing the pleasures of this world, we will never pursue the One who created it:

The love of money is a root of all sorts of evil, and some by longing for it have wandered away from the faith and pierced themselves with many griefs. But flee from these things, you man of God, and pursue righteousness, godliness, faith, love, perseverance and gentleness. Fight the good fight of faith; take hold of the eternal life to which you were called. (1 Timothy 6:10–12a)

Did you catch what Paul called the cause of "many griefs"? The "love of money," which can include material goods or prosperity in general. Contrary to the world's definition of suffering, real suffering occurs any time we find ourselves wandering away from faith in Christ. Here, Paul used the example of money/wealth, but it can just as easily be a relationship, fitness, or even reality TV. Anything that doesn't actively move us closer to God through Jesus Christ can lead to real suffering—the kind that's eternal and infinitely more dangerous than anything we can experience on earth.

This does not mean, of course, that all earthly suffering is a mirage, self-induced, or illegitimate. We've already explored the types of suffering we endure every day, and the Apostle Paul himself was no stranger to suffering during his life and ministry:

> Are they servants of Christ?—I speak as if insane—I more so; in far more labors, in far more imprisonments, beaten times without number, often in danger of death. Five times I received from the Jews thirty-nine lashes. Three times I was beaten with rods, once I was stoned, three times I was shipwrecked, a night and a day I have spent in the deep. I have been on frequent journeys, in dangers from rivers, dangers from robbers, dangers from my countrymen, dangers from the Gentiles, dangers in the city, dangers in the wilderness, dangers on the sea, dangers among false brethren; I have been in labor and hardship, through many sleepless nights, in hunger and thirst, often without food, in cold and exposure. (2 Corinthians 11:23–27)

Paul was well acquainted with suffering and experienced it more than any of us probably ever have or ever will. Physical, relational, emotional, spiritual, in nature—he encountered it all. Yet Jesus told him,

> "My grace is sufficient for you, for power is perfected in weakness." Most gladly, therefore, I [Paul] will rather boast about my weaknesses, so that the power of Christ may dwell in me. Therefore I am well content with weaknesses...for Christ's sake; for when I am weak, then I am strong. (2 Corinthians 12:9–10)

Suffering in this world is real, but it's also an opportunity either to move closer to God (His purpose for the suffering) or further away from Him (Satan's goal). Paul recognized that his weaknesses and struggles were ripe ground for God to accomplish powerful things in and through him. So while suffering was never fun, Paul could rejoice in it, knowing it served higher purposes both in his sanctification and the kingdom of God.

God uses suffering not only for our good, but ultimately for His glory. God is glorified when we, His children and created beings, choose to love, serve, and obey Him. Glorifying Him means to ascribe Him honor, worth, and praise. It means to worship and exalt Him—to put Him in His rightful place as Lord, Savior, and King. So how does our suffering bring Him glory? Earthly suffering glorifies God when we allow it to open our eyes to see Him more clearly as He is and respond accordingly.

For now we see in a mirror dimly, but then face to face; now I know in part, but then I will know fully just as I also have been fully known. (1 Corinthians 13:12)

But we all, with unveiled face, beholding as in a mirror the glory of the Lord, are being transformed into the same image from glory to glory, just as from the Lord, the Spirit. (2 Corinthians 3:18)

Whereas riches, comfort, and health act as dust that accumulates and blocks a proper perspective of God, suffering has a unique way of shining the spotlight on Him. It reminds us (sometimes quite potently) that this world is not our home, that we are but aliens and strangers in a foreign land, waiting to be reunited with our Savior. While grief and suffering are hardly enjoyable, the Christian has a unique opportunity to give it eternal significance in both the sanctification it ushers into our lives and the glory it ascribes to God.

We should not only expect suffering in this sin-contaminated world, but we should also embrace it. In his letter to the Philippian believers, Paul wrote, "For to me, to live is Christ, and to die is gain" (Philippians 1:21). The world attempts to ignore, fight, or avoid death and suffering as much as possible. But the Christian realizes that, while life on this earth is a gift, we should use it as a sacrifice to draw as many people to Christ as possible before we enter our true home and bask in God's glorious presence one day. Our death here, which is one hundred percent inevitable, is a blessed release from the chains of sin in this world and the beginning of unveiled life in Christ as we're united with Him in heaven.

It's futile for Christians to pursue ease, comfort, wealth, and safety on earth. That's simply not why we're here. Are any of those things bad? Absolutely not, and we can use them to glorify God. However, we should never pursue them to the point that they become the end for which we live. To do so is to misplace God completely as we remove Him from the center of our lives and hearts. Suffering is never fun, but "blessed is the man who perseveres under trial; for once he has been approved, he will receive the crown of life which the Lord has promised to those who love Him" (James 1:12).

Jesus and Suffering

God uses our suffering for His glory, but He does not call us to do something He has not already experienced a millionfold. Jesus is the ultimate example of suffering used both for humanity's good and God's ultimate glory.

While it's well-documented and understood that the pinnacle of Jesus's suffering took place on the cross (which we will explore), His suffering and grief did not begin there. Rather, they began where humanity's did—in the Garden of Eden. Read God's curse on the serpent after Adam and Eve sinned:

> I will put enmity between you and the woman, and between your seed and her seed; He shall bruise you on the head, and you shall bruise him on the heel. (Genesis 3:15)

The promise of suffering (the "bruise" Christ would endure on His heel) was given in the earliest days of creation. From this we learn two crucial points. First, as we've mentioned before, suffering is expected. Jesus knew before the creation of the world that He was going to suffer; it was a natural consequence of allowing created beings the capability of free choice. He knew the price He would pay to redeem the world He created. Nothing is a surprise to Jesus; nothing is unexpected or unprepared for.

Second, God suffered intense grief over mankind's sin long before the cross. Even in the early pages of Genesis, we read about His affliction:

> Then the LORD saw that the wickedness of man was great on the earth, and that every intent of the thoughts of his heart was only evil continually. The LORD was sorry that He had made man on the earth, and He was grieved in His heart. (Genesis 6:5–6)

Even though mankind's sin was not a surprise, it still made God's heart ache to the point that He decided to start over with a global flood. And grief is not the only emotion God experiences over sin. He gets angry,[23] feels metaphorically sick,[24] experiences enmity with man,[25] and more. Thus, God suffered from the effects of mankind's sin long before His remedy to redeem them on the cross.

Yet even in all the grief we've caused Him over the centuries, God still loves us, forgives us, and wants to spend eternity with us. This, of course, is why Jesus chose to go to the cross. It's why He willingly experienced the most excruciating form of suffering the world has ever known. The cross was the culmination of His suffering and arguably the most potent example of suffering that's ever occurred.

As with our suffering, Jesus's suffering on the cross was multifaceted. The physical component of His suffering is most obvious and well-known. Mel Gibson's *The Passion of the Christ* did a good job of capturing people's attention on this subject, but it did not go far enough. In the movie, Jesus was still recognizable, even in His last moments on the cross. More than that, He was still recognizable as a man. He still had His beard, He still retained most of the skin on His face and body, etc. Scripture, however, tells us that Jesus was beaten so badly, He was not just unrecognizable as Himself. He was also unrecognizable as a person.

> Just as many were astonished at you, My people, so
> His appearance was marred more than any man, and
> His form more than the sons of men. (Isaiah 52:14)

Jesus's physical suffering was so intense that it marred His entire appearance and made Him completely unrecognizable. All the children's Bible story books with tiny blood trickles falling from Jesus's head, hands, and feet, while admittedly age appropriate, are grossly inaccurate. Before He even went to the cross, Jesus's beatings were so severe that most (if not all) the flesh of His back was ripped off. Carson describes the intensity of this thrashing:

> The victim was stripped and tied to a post, and then
> beaten by several torturers (in the Roman provinces
> they were soldiers) until they were exhausted, or

their commanding officer called them off. For victims who, like Jesus, were neither Roman citizens nor soldiers, the favoured instrument was a whip whose leather thongs were fitted with pieces of bone or lead or other metal. The beatings were so savage that the victims sometimes died. Eyewitness records report that such brutal scourgings could leave victims with their bones and entrails exposed.[26]

Jesus endured this brutality before He went to the cross. In fact, such beatings prior to crucifixions were intentionally designed to speed up the victim's death, especially in instances when crucifixions were held so close to Passover. Neither the Romans nor Jews wanted the victim's death dragging on so long that it would interfere with Passover, so with vicious beatings, they hastened the death as much as possible.[27]

It is little wonder Jesus was incapable of carrying His own cross. He did not have the physical capacity, stamina, or wherewithal to do much of anything by that point. It's quite surprising He was even conscious.

The crucifixion itself bore its own physical agony. As is commonly known, nails were driven into Christ's hands (most likely, wrists) and feet before the cross was erected, and He hung until He died. A relatively unknown fact is that the cause of death from most crucifixions was asphyxiation. Hanging without any support except nails (assisted sometimes by ropes fastened to their arms), made it difficult to breathe. Victims/criminals would need to push down on their pierced feet in order to prop themselves up enough to fill their lungs with air. This process could take days, but eventually, the criminal would simply run out of energy to push themselves up, and thus, would suffocate. If the torturers were in a rush (or if the criminals were Jewish, who did not believe in allowing bodies to hang overnight), they hastened the death by breaking the criminals' legs so they couldn't push themselves up anymore. We know they were in a hurry with Jesus, because they made His suffering so immense prior to the cross, but this tactic was obsolete. He was dead before they needed to break His legs, which is why they ended up piercing His side with a spear (John 19:34).

Jesus endured one of most gruesome forms of pain one can possibly imagine. While this section included only a brief overview of the physical aspects of His suffering, I hope it shed light on its reality while exposing the exceptionally downplayed versions too often portrayed in books, sermons, and songs today.

The physical component of Jesus's suffering is certainly the most well-known, but He suffered in other areas as well, including relationally, with both man and God the Father. (We'll explore the latter in more depth when we discuss His spiritual suffering.) But make no mistake: the cross was relationally agonizing for Jesus. He was brutally murdered by people He loved and came to save. While some remained loyal and grieved for Him during the trial, beatings, sentencing, and crucifixion, more of them mocked, insulted, and hated Him. Read these short verses for a glimpse into a few ways people turned against Him:

Some began to spit on Him, and to blindfold Him, and to beat Him with their fists…And the officers received Him with slaps in the face. (Mark 14:65)

They kept beating His head with a reed, and spitting on Him, and kneeling and bowing before Him. (Mark 15:19)

And Herod with his soldiers, after treating Him with contempt and mocking Him, dressed Him in a gorgeous robe and sent Him back to Pilate. (Luke 23:11)

But they kept on calling out, saying, "Crucify, crucify Him!"… But they were insistent, with loud voices asking that He be crucified. And their voices began to prevail. (Luke 23:21, 23)

And the people stood by, looking on. And even the rulers were sneering at Him, saying, "He saved others; let Him save Himself if this is the Christ of God, His Chosen One." The soldiers also mocked Him. (Luke 23:35–36a)

Then they spat in His face and beat Him with their fists; and others slapped Him. (Matthew 26:67)

Pilate said to them, "Then what shall I do with Jesus who is called Christ?" They all said, "Crucify Him!" And he said, "Why, what evil has He done?" But they kept shouting all the more, saying, "Crucify Him!"

When Pilate saw that he was accomplishing nothing, but rather that a riot was starting, he took water and washed his hands in front of the crowd, saying, "I am innocent of this Man's blood; see to that yourselves." And all the people said, "His blood shall be on us and on our children!" (Matthew 27:22–25)

You get the idea. The priests, scribes, and Pharisees had always hated Jesus out of jealousy, but they stirred up the masses against Him as well. Mob psychology is real and dangerous. For reasons still not entirely understood, people do things in large groups they would never do on their own. A silly example is that of sporting events—men (and women) paint their half-naked bodies and scream their throats raw over a game that will never bear any kind of eternal or even earthly significance.

A more solemn example is the Salem Witch Trials of 1692. At the flimsy, unsubstantiated testimony of a couple of girls who claimed to be victims of witches, one hundred and fifty people were imprisoned and twenty-five were killed. The Holocaust is perhaps the most widely known example of mob mentality—millions of Jews were brutally imprisoned and/or murdered because of the prejudice of one man manipulating the masses. The point here is that relationships are powerful and influential. The crowds turned against Jesus just days after welcoming Him into their city with palm branches and praise.

One often-overlooked miracle of the cross (especially in light of this relational component) is that Jesus stayed there. Would you? If I'm honest, I doubt I would have. Yet there hung

Jesus—blood pouring out from his head, back, hands, and feet, each drop slowly draining life from the Giver of Life. Each convulsion of pain, each groan, each breath causing a new wave of knife-like agony was mocked by those who put Him there. Little did they know the blood draining life from His body would be the blood that would infuse life into theirs. His only escape was death, and while He could have ended His life at any moment to hasten the process, He didn't. He hung there, on the brink of death for hours…all because He wanted a relationship with us. More than that, He wanted our relationship with Him to thrive and last for eternity. Jesus did not cave to fleshly desires, nor did He turn on those who so easily turned on Him. The relational aspect of His suffering was intense that day as He endured the hatred, scorn, and malice of those He was giving His life for.

In addition to physical and relational suffering, Jesus also experienced emotional suffering. Before going to the cross, He was in such agony in Gethsemane that "His sweat became like drops of blood, falling down upon the ground" (Luke 22:44). I've experienced some ups and downs, but I've never been in such agony that I sweat drops like blood. This emotional turmoil was due partly to the fact that He knew what was coming. He prayed, "Father, if You are willing, remove this cup from Me" (Luke 22:42). Unlike most people, who rarely have any idea something bad is about to befall them, Jesus knew exactly what He faced. He knew down to every last gory detail what was to come during His trials, sentencing, and crucifixion. He also understood that He would have to endure separation from His Father. He did not want to go to the cross; no sane person would. But He did it with eyes wide open, knowing the immense cost He'd have to pay, as well as the eternal opportunities it would open for those who chose to follow Him. As He told His disciples about His impending death in the gospel of John:

> "Now My soul has become troubled; and what shall I say, 'Father, save Me from this hour'? But for this purpose I came to this hour. Father, glorify Your name." Then a voice came out of heaven: "I have both glorified it, and will glorify it again." (John 12:27–28)

Physical, relational, and emotional suffering are all awful on their own, but they are never isolated from each other, our souls, or our bodies. The culmination of spiritual suffering was the cross. Because He was God incarnate and knew no sin, Jesus was never separated from God while He was alive on earth. He never did anything to warrant God's wrath. This feat was necessary in order to qualify Him to be the ultimate sacrificial lamb for humanity. While His temptation to sin was real (and arguably more intense than any temptation we'll ever experience, because we cave so easily), He remained pure, spotless, and blameless so He could offer that status to us through His death (Hebrews 7:23–28). He experienced suffering in many areas before the cross, but the cross was the apex of all possible suffering, for on it Jesus endured the eternal wrath of God.

The author of Hebrews writes, "It is a terrifying thing to fall into the hands of the living God" (Hebrews 10:31). God's wrath is not to be dumbed down, muted, or trifled with. While we were already under the wrath of God before accepting Jesus as our Savior (Ephesians 2:3), we have not experienced a fraction of the wrath that awaits those who die apart from Him. Nor have we experienced the full wrath of God that Jesus endured while on the cross:

> He was despised and forsaken of men, a man of sorrows and acquainted with grief; and like one from whom men hide their face He was despised, and we did not esteem Him. Surely our griefs He Himself bore, and our sorrows He carried; yet we ourselves esteemed Him stricken, smitten of God, and afflicted. But He was pierced through for our transgressions, He was crushed for our iniquities; the chastening for our well-being fell upon Him, and by His scourging we are healed. But the LORD was pleased to crush Him, putting Him to grief, if He would render Himself as a guilt offering, He will see His offspring...As a result of the anguish of His soul, He will see it and be satisfied; by His knowledge the Righteous One, My Servant, will justify the many, as He will bear their iniquities. (Isaiah 53:3–5, 10a, 11).

When Jesus took our place—when He bore the punishment for *our* sins—He experienced spiritual agony to degrees we literally cannot comprehend. Both Matthew and Mark record the most torturous words ever uttered in the history of the world: "My God, My God, why have You forsaken Me?"[28] God turned His face, favor, and peace away from Christ on the cross. His stance toward Him was reflected in the darkness that consumed the world as Jesus hung there to die. Unlike sinners who are blind in their depravity prior to coming to the gospel (and still don't see completely clearly afterward), Jesus knew and felt the full heaviness of humanity's depravity as He endured God's wrath.

And He endured it all willingly:

> For while we were still helpless, at the right time Christ died for the ungodly. For one will hardly die for a righteous man; though perhaps for the good man someone would dare even to die. But God demonstrates His own love toward us, in that while we were yet sinners, Christ died for us. Much more then, having now been justified by His blood, we shall be saved from the wrath of God through Him. For if while we were enemies we were reconciled to God through the death of His Son, much more, having been reconciled, we shall be saved by His life. And not only this, but we also exult in God through our Lord Jesus Christ, through whom we have now received the reconciliation. (Romans 5:6–11)

Jesus's suffering was unlike any the earth has ever known, and He endured it all for us. His suffering served the greatest purposes of all—the fulfillment of the gospel and an invitation for mankind to be reconciled with God.

Because of Jesus's suffering and the sin-infested world we still live in, we cannot be surprised when we encounter suffering. Nor should we ever allow it to interfere with, stunt, or diminish our faith. Jesus kept His eyes on His Father and the gospel until the very end, giving us the best example we could ever attempt to follow.

Friends, don't be fooled by the lies of the prosperity gospel or other erroneous theological conclusions. Bad things happen to everyone; neither the quality nor quantity of our faith shields us from the devastating consequences of sin in this world. We should also not be consumed with fighting suffering (for ourselves or others) to the point that we despair or refuse to accept the reality of sin. This world will never again be Eden; it will never be our true home. However, we have hope in the meantime. We know that while God allows suffering to come, He also gives us His Spirit to help us endure it. The Lord uses our suffering to strengthen our faith and lift His name on high. If we keep our eyes on Jesus, the Author and Perfecter of our faith, we will endure any and every type of suffering with a peace that surpasses all understanding.

> In the world you have tribulation, but take courage;
> I have overcome the world. (John 16:33)

Chapter Seven
Justice (Fairness/Equality)

Myth:

Jesus came for justice and was a great equalizer. He came to make all things fair to everyone, and He wanted all people to be equal.

The Truth Within the Myth:

Jesus did come for justice, and we are all equally image-bearers of God.

Where Truth Gets Distorted by a Lie:

Justice is one of the biggest, if not the biggest hype word of the last decade in our country. People rise up and demand justice for countless issues—race, gender, "rights," retributions, oppression, and more. People want what they think they deserve, and the enemy milks that cow for all it's worth. As with the other topics we've discussed thus far, the concept of justice is rooted in our worldview. Satan has warped the world's perspective to keep it from aligning with God's as much as possible. To explore justice, then, we need to dig deep through numerous layers of mental, societal, and spiritual sediment to discover what it really is. Unsurprisingly, the world's definition of justice does not align with God's, and He's not the One who needs to change.

Our discussion will begin with a brief note about identity and justice. Then we'll define biblical justice, explore what biblical justice looks like in this world, consider social justice, and conclude with a segment on Jesus and justice.

Identity and Justice

Before tackling a difficult, sensitive, and highly emotional topic, we must first state a foundational truth that will set the stage for a productive analysis. As Christians, we are to define ourselves and each other *first* by our identity in Christ (which we'll delve into specifically in the next chapter). Every other descriptor is not only secondary in position but also in importance. No other qualifier or adjective we use to describe ourselves comes close to that of our identity in Christ, which is secured through the gospel and impenetrable by anything in this world.

Why is this important? Because far too many of us describe ourselves with an adjective *before* the term Christian, and this perspective is grossly unbiblical. For example, some may refer to themselves as black Christians. Or, as is becoming more commonplace in today's society, using several monikers—a liberal, lesbian, Asian Christian (the validity of which is a discussion for another time) or other multiple descriptors. The point here is that, as Christians, we are to identify as "Christ- followers" first and foremost, and resolve to ground our identity—and every aspect of our identity—in Christ.

In 2 Corinthians 5:17, the Apostle Paul wrote, "Therefore if anyone is in Christ, he is a new creature; the old things passed away; behold, new things have come." When we enter salvation through Jesus, we are completely transformed. We may look the same on the outside, but "our inner man is being renewed day by day" (2 Corinthians 4:16). We encounter a radical shift in our person as well as our perspective and goal in life. From the moment of salvation, our purpose in life is to glorify God and enjoy Him forever. While we are graciously provided with numerous ventures in which to pursue this goal, the goal itself can never be compromised for the sake of the ventures.

This is crucial to understand regarding any issue—theological, political, social, cultural, etc. Scripture is not a piece of literature we add to our library. It's the framework from which we view the rest of our library. Thus, in order to understand justice properly, we must first understand it as God does. If we find our views contradict God's, it's our responsibility to reject our erroneous, gospel-contrary views and align them with His correct ones. We must be willing to sacrifice every adjective we're tempted to place before the term Christian and strive to live up to that term first and foremost.

Practically, this means that while we align our definitions with God's, we must also align our hearts and passions with His.

We are not at liberty to pursue agendas that run opposite of God's, regardless of how appealing or emotionally satisfying they may seem. Case in point: women's "rights," particularly those supporting abortion. Some women may be tempted to identify themselves as feminist Christians pursuing "justice" in demanding that all women have the right to choose what they do with their own bodies, even if it means aborting an unborn child. This is not even on the spectrum of possibility for genuine Christians living in submission to Christ. Scripture is crystal clear about the value of human life—to take an innocent one is murder. That fact doesn't change, regardless of the powerful emotional incentives argued by feminists. Likewise, Christians must emphatically reject any agenda, policy, worldview, perspective, or idea that does not align with God's Word.

Biblical Justice

I dislike using adjectives in front of topics addressed in Scripture (Biblical this or Biblical that), because each should stand on its own as God's mandate. God is the Creator and Sustainer of the universe. He needs no adjectives. However, since humanity has added adjectives to His truth in order to redefine and corrupt it, we will use the phrase "biblical justice" to communicate what God means by the concept of justice in Scripture.

Biblical justice begins with God, for it is an extension of who God is, much like love. Justice, also like love, is not synonymous with God. Rather, it's an integral part of His character. He can no more be separated from justice than He could be separated from Himself. Justice is an extension of His rightness, holiness, and perfection.

> The Rock! His work is perfect, for all His ways are just; a God of faithfulness and without injustice, righteous and upright is He. (Deuteronomy 32:4)

> For he who does wrong will receive the consequences of the wrong which he has done, and that without partiality. (Colossians 3:25)

> Now then, let the fear of the LORD be upon you; be very careful what you do, for the LORD our God will have no part in unrighteousness or partiality or the taking of a bribe. (2 Chronicles 19:7)

> For the LORD your God is the God of gods and the Lord of lords, the great, the mighty, and the awesome God who does not show partiality nor take a bribe. He executes justice for the orphan and the widow, and shows His love for the alien by giving him food and clothing. (Deuteronomy 10:17–18)

> He loves righteousness and justice; the earth is full of the lovingkindness of the LORD. (Psalm 33:5)

> For there is no partiality with God. (Romans 2:11)

> Your throne, O God, is forever and ever; a scepter of uprightness is the scepter of Your kingdom. (Psalm 45:6)

You get the idea. Justice is spoken of hundreds of times throughout Scripture, both in reference to God and in what He expects from His people. So justice comes from God…but what exactly is it?

Simply put, *justice is the impartial exercise of righteousness as determined by God (in His Word) in a situation or relationship.* In other words, *justice is when things are as they should be.* This refers to relationships and situations that either currently operate the way they should (i.e., justice is currently being carried out properly), or when force is introduced to make them be what they should be (retribution or punishment is introduced to right a particular wrong). The most crucial point to clarify about this definition, though, is that the "should" in "the way things *should* be" is not subjective. *We* do not get to define how things should be according to our own terms, ideas, opinions, preferences, or ideologies. The "should" is and will eternally be defined by God as stated in His Word.

God is truth (Isaiah 65:16) and the ultimate authority (John 17:2). He is also righteous (Psalm 11:7). This means He is perfect, holy, and right in every way. Thus, not only is God just, but He is also the perfect executor of justice, making and keeping both relationships and situations "right" in His gospel plan. Our responsibility and privilege as His children is to obey, follow, and trust Him according to the laws and principles He's provided us in His Word.

Biblical Justice in the World

God carries out His justice in numerous ways—eternally and temporally, spiritually and physically, personally and nationally, politically and even within nature. Sometimes His execution of justice is obvious (the flood account in Genesis 6–8), while at other times, it occurs behind the veil, and we have to trust He has it under control (the Esther narrative). But no matter how, when, or where God executes justice, it is *His* justice being carried out in *His* perfect way according to *His* sovereign plan.

God may not execute justice in a way (or within a timeframe) that we think He should. This does not mean He hasn't or won't carry it out:

> For we know Him who said, "Vengeance is Mine, I will repay." And again, "The Lord will judge His people." (Hebrews 10:30)

> But do not let this one fact escape your notice, beloved, that with the Lord one day is like a thousand years, and a thousand years like one day. The Lord is not slow about His promise, as some count slowness, but is patient toward you, not wishing for any to perish, but for all to come to repentance. (2 Peter 3:8–9)

Those last verses provide us with the reason God hasn't unleased another global disaster like the flood: He is patient, "not willing for any to perish, but for all to come to repentance." Don't miss this: God currently allows injustice to occur on earth (just as He allows sin) so more people can come to repentance and salvation in Jesus Christ. If God righted every wrong this very minute, the world would cease to be:

> But by His word the present heavens and earth are being reserved for fire, kept for the day of judgment and destruction of ungodly men...the day of the Lord will come like a thief, in which the heavens will pass away with a roar and the elements will be destroyed with intense heat, and the earth and its works will be burned up. (2 Peter 3:7, 10)

In other words, it's actually a *good* thing that God has not righted every injustice on earth! His patience gives us more time to participate in His gospel plan and draw people to Him.

A major fallacy of most justice-on-earth activists is their attempt (whether consciously or not) to create some kind of Edenic utopia. Their goal is to bring heaven to earth, not by way of carrying out the gospel according to God's will, but by creating a society that's so self-sufficient, it doesn't need God anymore. While self-sufficiency can be an admirable goal to some extent (a grown adult not mooching off his parents, for example), it is neither admirable nor remotely possible on a societal level because of our sin nature. Thomas Sowell once said, "The vision of the left, and I think many conservatives underestimate this, is really a more attractive vision in itself. The only reason for not believing in it is that it does not work...if the world were the way the left conceives it to be, it would be a better world than the way the right conceives it to be. It just happens that the world is not that way."[29] An Edenic utopia on earth is simply not possible anymore.

As Christians, we know the reason for that is sin—the depravity that corrupts every person, animal, and the earth itself. "For all have sinned and fall short of the glory of God" (Romans 3:23). For centuries, people have tried to save themselves—some through legalism and keeping the rules, and others by pursuing their own "truth" and letting the chips fall where they will. But it has never worked. Not even close. That's one reason our guard should always go up when we hear about a proposed solution, policy, initiative, movement, or governmental mandate that claims to solve the problem of injustice in the world. Justice—the perfect execution of righteousness according to truth—cannot be realized in this world. It's impossible. While all things are possible with God, this is something He said will remain impossible (in totality) until this earth passes away. Justice will be a reality in the new heavens and new earth. It's just not an attainable reality for us in the here and now:

> But according to His promise we are looking for new heavens and a new earth, in which righteousness dwells. (2 Peter 3:13)

Because justice will never be fully realized on this earth, should we, as Christians, simply ignore it? Should we stand idly by and allow injustice to consume every aspect of our families, society, and world? Absolutely not. In fact, God demands that we do the opposite:

He has told you, O man, what is good; and what does the LORD require of you but to do justice, to love kindness, and to walk humbly with your God? (Micah 6:8)

We Christians need to live up to our name. Who we are and Whom we belong to is supposed to dictate what we do with our lives. Thus, justice (upholding God's righteous law) is a natural byproduct of the Holy Spirit dwelling in our hearts.

Did you catch that? Doing good and pursuing biblical justice is a *byproduct* and *result* of living a Christ-centered life. It is not, nor should it ever be, the *ultimate goal* of a believer. This is especially true considering the fact that, as just discussed, we can't fully accomplish it in this life anyway. Satan leads Christians astray by enticing us to exchange the *ultimate* (Christ-centered, gospel-driven lives) for the socially deemed *urgent* issues of injustice today. Along with confusing believers regarding the definition of biblical justice (as opposed to social, healing, racial, and other agendas labeled as justice), he is doing everything possible to separate and prioritize injustice over and beyond the gospel. Fighting perceived or actual injustice in the world has become the goal of many believers, to the extent that many of us sacrifice truth and the gospel itself along the way.

Social Justice

Time and space will not permit exploring every "type" of justice society advocates today. But one type worth exposing in light of God's truth is social justice, for it continues to wreak astronomical havoc on society as well as churches.

The Oxford Dictionary defines social justice as:

> Justice in terms of the distribution of wealth, opportunities, and privileges within a society: individuality gives way to the struggle for social justice.

In other words, social justice is the redistribution of resources by the state to those they deem "oppressed." Social justice advocates prioritized equity (a desired *outcome*) over equality (equal *opportunities*). The Interaction Institute for Social Change uses the following graphic to help distinguish between equality and equity[30]:

EQUALITY | **EQUITY**

While this may look good, reasonable, and fair at first glance, it is actually utterly misleading, narrow-minded, and most definitely not biblical.

Notice equality, which can be defined as "the state of being equal, especially in status, rights, or opportunities."[31] In other words, equality is when everyone in society is given equal rights and opportunities under the law. Neither partiality nor prejudice exists. Two people with the same criminal background who admit guilt to the same crime will get the same punishment. In the same way, two people who are equally qualified for a position within a company have the exact same chance of being hired. That's equality. Everyone has the same opportunities (the same "box" in the image above) and can do with them what they will.[32]

Equity, however, focuses not on opportunity, but on outcome. As shown in the image above, the goal of equity is based on results—every person, regardless of height, must have the same view of the ballgame. The only way to accomplish this is by taking the box away from one and giving it to someone else who isn't as tall. While this may seem fair on the surface, it is anything but fair, especially according to biblical principles. Equity is actually *injustice* in several ways.

Fundamentally, equity defies the tenth commandment: you shall not covet (Exodus 20:17). The entire premise of equity is comprised of being jealous for something that someone else has (a better "view," higher status, more wealth, etc.). Rather than being content with what we have (Philippians 4:11), one person (or a group of people) decides he/she wants what someone else has. Yet it doesn't stop there. While it's not inherently wrong to want something, we cross a line when we: 1) feel we "deserve" it, 2) are not willing to work for it, 3) accuse and attack others in order to get it, and 4) make good things *ultimate* things.

Let's start with number one. We think we "deserve" what someone else has. Social justice advocates claim that this generation of certain minority groups "deserves" material perks from the government and society at large because their ancestors were sinned against. Were they sinned against? Absolutely, and horrendously, just as people still experience today all over the world (which social justice advocates tend to ignore). However, special favor should never be bestowed through guilt—especially superficial, unwarranted guilt imposed upon people who never participated in the sins of their ancestors. Claiming minorities deserve unmerited, unearned favor as an inherent right, especially when taken from someone else, flies in the face of biblical principles and freedom in general.

Many issues arise with this agenda, like the fact that slavery in America was extremely brief compared to the rest of the world and history at large. Also, slave owners were both white *and black*, rendering the entire premise of restitutions from white people alone today completely unwarranted.[33] But most importantly, this line of thinking is validated nowhere in Scripture. In fact, the exact opposite is true. The only thing we all deserve as fallen human beings is to rot in hell for eternity. Sounds harsh, but that's exactly what our sin requires, save the grace of God through Jesus on the cross. Anything and everything in our lives that's better than hell (which is everything) is given to us by the grace of God, and we should thank Him for it constantly. If fairness is the equal distribution of what we deserve, we'd all receive a non-refundable, nonstop ticket straight to hell.

That, of course, doesn't preach well, so the truth is ignored. Worse, sparks of covetousness are fanned into flames by well-meaning, utterly misguided individuals who grossly misunderstand the gospel. Coveting after things we don't have, yet think we deserve, is not only theologically erroneous, but it's also irreverent. By doing so, we tell God that 1) we are not thankful for the myriad of blessings He *has* gifted us with, like good health, clothing, jobs, food, family, etc., and 2) that the gospel, that *He,* isn't enough to give us joy and contentment. Our circumstances should never dictate our attitude, perspective, or relationship with God. He is and should always be the object of our desire and the fulfillment of our souls:

> To be with Christ is to be in heaven, and to be in heaven is to be with Christ. That prisoner of the Lord very sweetly writes in one of his glowing letters, "O my Lord Jesus Christ, if I could be in heaven without you, it would be a hell; and if I could be in hell, and have you still, it would be a heaven to me, for you are all the heaven I want." It is true, is it not, Christian? Does not your soul say so?...All you need to make you blessed, supremely blessed, is to be with Christ.[34]

Our hearts should desire and move toward Christ, regardless of our circumstances. Remember Job. He was "blameless, upright, fearing God and turning away from evil" (Job 1:1). He was also very wealthy and blessed with a large family. He consistently sacrificed offerings to God in the event that his children might have sinned against Him in their hearts. Satan accused him of basically using God to get blessings, so He gave Satan permission to afflict Job. Satan ended up taking all his material wealth, killing all of his children, and eventually striking Job with excruciatingly painful boils. Yet even in losing everything, "Job did not sin with his lips" (Job 2:10); rather, he worshipped God.

Job recognized what many of us (especially social justice advocates) forget: that we deserve absolutely nothing good on this earth. If anyone deserved material blessings, it was Job. He lived righteously, worked hard, loved his family, and was a dedicated follower of God. He didn't ride the coattails of a previous generation's blessings or hardships. Nor did he think his righteous living afforded him a life of luxury. He praised God in abundance and with nothing, and when destitution fell upon him, he never once dishonored or sinned against God.

Today, however, more and more people grow discontent with what they have. In addition to erroneously believing they "deserve" more, they fall prey to issue number two: they're not willing to work for what they want. This exposes another major sin of the social justice movement, which is laziness. Under the guise of "retributive justice" for sins committed against ancestors in centuries past, many social justice advocates believe the "oppressed" should not have to work (or at least not as hard as others) to receive extra income or opportunities. There's actually an initiative that claims people with increased levels of melanin in their skin deserve to nap more because their ancestors couldn't. Thus, they (not their ancestors) have earned the right to rest more, work less, and receive the same (if not, more) pay than other working ethnicities.[35]

God created us to work, and labor was well established before the fall introduced sin into the world (Genesis 2:15). When we work, and work well, we bring glory to God (Colossians 3:23). Laziness, thus, is an affront to God, and Scripture has much to say about its condemnation:

> Like vinegar to the teeth and smoke to the eyes, so is the lazy one to those who send him. (Proverbs 10:26)

> The way of the lazy is as a hedge of thorns, but the path of the upright is a highway. (Proverbs 15:19)

> Laziness casts into a deep sleep, and an idle man will suffer hunger. (Proverbs 19:15)

> The soul of the sluggard craves and gets nothing, but the soul of the diligent is made fat. (Proverbs 13:4)

> He also who is slack in his work is brother to him who destroys. (Proverbs 18:9)

> If anyone is not willing to work, then he is not to eat, either. (2 Thessalonians 3:10b)

Much more could be said, but the principle remains the same: laziness will never meet God's approval. Those who desire additional material blessings and are not willing to work for them are acting in defiance against God's Word.

Third, social justice advocates thrive on attacking and shaming others (namely, white people) in an effort to get what they want. Voddie Baucham Jr. does a brilliant job of describing the "sins" of white people as articulated by social justice theorists in the following points:

1. First, white people created whiteness, which is defined as "a set of normative privileges granted to white-skinned individuals and groups which is 'invisible' to those privileged by it."[36] Another definition provided by Darrel B. Harrison in the "Just Thinking" Podcast is that whiteness is "anything that's not blackness."[37]

2. White people also created white privilege, which is defined as "a series of unearned advantages that accrue to white people by virtue of their whiteness."[38]

3. Then they created white supremacy, which is "any belief, behavior, or system that supports, promotes, or enhances white privilege."[39]

4. Next, they created white complicity, which is how "white people, through the practices of whiteness and by benefiting from white privilege, contribute to the maintenance of systemic racial injustice."[40]

5. Then they created white equilibrium, which is "the belief system that allows white people to remain comfortably ignorant."[41]

6. Lastly, white people created white fragility, which is "the inability and unwillingness of white people to talk about race due to the grip that whiteness, white supremacy, white privilege, white complicity, and white equilibrium exert on them (knowingly or unknowingly)."[42]

As is hopefully quite apparent, white people are the targets of social justice theorists' attacks and, as some have said, cannot win or make amends that minorities would ever approve. If white people deny being racist, they're labeled delusional. Yet admitting and/or repenting of their whiteness is not enough either. They must live in a constant state of repentance and give without measure in order to recompense for their unknown sins as well as the sins of their ancestors.

These attacks and negative perspectives based solely on a group's skin color are not only (quite ironically) racist, but also completely unbiblical:

> For you are all sons of God through faith in Christ Jesus. For all of you who were baptized into Christ have clothed yourselves with Christ. There is neither Jew nor Greek, there is neither slave nor free man, there is neither male nor female; for you are all one in Christ Jesus. (Galatians 3:26–28)

Christians should never attack one another, period. We are to use discernment and call out legitimate sins among our brothers and sisters when we see them (Matthew 18), but we are never to hate subjectively or harbor bitterness toward people. We are all "one in Christ Jesus." Misguided efforts of social justice theorists dig deeper fissures in the body of Christ, defaming His name, crippling the gospel's movement in the world, and accomplishing Satan's agenda in spades.

While much more can be said (and has been in numerous well-articulated volumes written by others),[43] a final point worth noting again is that social justice theorists error by prioritizing good things as *ultimate* things. Of course it's applaudable to want equality (not equity) for all people and to advocate that the law and other social constructs should be executed fairly and without discrimination among all members of society. However, this initiative, especially for Christians, is not the *ultimate* goal. We are but aliens and strangers[44] in this world, whose goal is to "proclaim the excellencies of Him who has called you out of darkness into His marvelous light" (1 Peter 2:9b). As the Apostle John rightfully noted, "the world is passing away, and also its lusts; but the one who does the will of God lives forever" (1 John 2:17).

Therefore, desiring and advocating biblical justice is admirable if pursued in accordance with His will. But to expect the completion or fruition of justice in this world reveals a heart set on earth, not on God or His gospel.

Jesus and Justice

Many people claim that Jesus came for justice and was a great equalizer—that He came to make all things fair, and lifted up the downtrodden in society to put them on equal standing with the well off. Some of that is true, but as with all other lies of the enemy, much of it is not and can be dangerously misleading.

In one sense, Jesus absolutely came for justice. We can argue that Jesus *is* justice—the most perfect manifestation of justice the world has ever known. He did, in fact, come to die on the cross for our sin, to satisfy God's uncompromising demand for adequate payment of sin. "The wages of sin is death," and Jesus paid that price with His life on the cross (Romans 3:23).

Thus, Jesus's sacrifice was the epitome of cosmic justice. He righted all wrongs between God and those who would repent and believe. But this justice was for His kingdom; it was never intended to be perfect, situational justice in this world.

Regarding fairness and equality, Jesus absolutely embodied both in that He extends the offer of salvation to everyone without bias. He provides everyone with an equal opportunity to come to God through His sacrifice on the cross:

> God "desires all men to be saved and to come to the knowledge of the truth. For there is one God, and one mediator also between God and men, the man Christ Jesus, who gave Himself as a ransom for all..." (1 Timothy 2:4–6a)

Now, a couple of objections could be made regarding this point, namely predestination and the question, "What about those who've never heard about Jesus?" Regarding the first, predestination is a theological fact whereby God predestines or preordains some people for salvation:

> For those whom He foreknew, He also predestined to become conformed to the image of His Son, so that He would be the firstborn among many brethren; and these whom He predestined, He also called; and these whom He called, He also justified; and these whom He justified, He also glorified. (Romans 8:29–30)

He predestined us to adoption as sons through Jesus

Christ to Himself, according to the kind intention
of His will (Ephesians 1:5)

At first glance, this does not sound very "fair," for if God
purposely ordains some for salvation, that means others are
left out and are destined to hell. But we must remember one
crucial fact we've discussed before—if God were truly fair, *all*
humanity would be destined to hell. Fairness would require
that our sins receive what they deserve: separation from God
and eternity spent in hell away from Him. The fact that God
saves *any* is a miracle, and that's exactly what He did through
Jesus. Jesus made it possible for all to be saved, knowing full
well that only a select, preordained number would respond to
His call. The invitation is extended to all.

The second objection often heard is, "What about those who
have never heard about Jesus or the gospel?" Surely, it's not
"fair" for them to them to go to hell if they had no
opportunity to hear about Him. Aside from our previous
point that all deserve to go to hell, the Apostle Paul answers
this objection clearly in Romans 1:18–20:

> For the wrath of God is revealed from heaven against
> all ungodliness and unrighteousness of men who
> suppress the truth in unrighteousness, because that
> which is known about God is evident within them;
> for God made it evident to them. For since the
> creation of the world His invisible attributes, His
> eternal power and divine nature, have been clearly
> seen, being understood through what has been
> made, so that they are without excuse.

In other words, we are all guilty, without excuse, utterly depraved, and deserving of hell. Our eternal damnation would be justice exacted. Fortunately, God is most certainly not fair; rather, He is entirely gracious and extends the unmerited invitation of salvation to all who believe through His Son, Jesus Christ.[45]

Jesus advocates equality (equal opportunity for all to come to Him), but does not advocate equity (taking from "the oppressors" in order to give to "the oppressed"). Not once did Jesus take from some in order to give to others. Politically, this would have regarded the Roman government, the ones in political power when He lived on earth. When people complain about the "oppression" of our American government, I wince a bit at the naivete of that claim. Of all the governments since the beginning of time, oppression in the United States is balmy. During Christ's time on earth, the Roman government was tolerant of other religions and cultures but maintained complete control over their subjects. Government officials could do what they wanted, largely without fear of retribution. It was a top-down society, certainly not run by the people for the people.

Consider Jesus's cousin, John the Baptist, who was beheaded simply because he (correctly) accused Herod of immorality (Matthew 14:1–12). Did John the Baptist deserve to die for that? Was his punishment at all fair? Nope. But notice something about that narrative: Jesus did not interfere or intervene. He could've easily saved John. He could have gotten him out of prison in the blink of an eye and protected him from harm. But He didn't usurp the unjust political hierarchy that sent John to an early grave. He didn't deliver the oppressed from injustice and punish the oppressor for his gross abuse of power. And John was His cousin!

Jesus didn't bother Himself with politics because the kingdom He was establishing was not of this world. He did not come to liberate the Jews from the Roman government, much to many of the disciples' dismay. Instead, He advocated submission and obedience to the government. Despite its despicable injustices, Jesus instructed His followers to pay taxes to the Roman government: "'Render to Caesar the things that are Caesar's, and to God the things that are God's'" (Mark 12:17a). Thus, no modern-day Christian can accurately claim Jesus advocated for equity in the political realm.

The political realm was not the only area Jesus abstained from pursuing equity. In fact, He didn't do so in any aspect of life, either on earth or in heaven. Consider His healing ministry. He encountered thousands upon thousands of people in His ministry, and though He healed many, He didn't heal everyone, which is what equity would demand. Further, He didn't provide them with jobs or financial security afterward. Why is that significant? Many of those Jesus healed had been sick a long time and had no clue how to make a living, apart from begging. Unemployment checks did not exist back then. If you didn't work, you didn't eat. The two exceptions were having family or friends who provided for you or begging. If someone was healed, however, they would receive no further pity, and thus, no money.

Consider the ill man who had lived with his immobilizing infirmity for thirty-eight years (John 5:2–15). Jesus asked him what seems to be a silly question: "Do you wish to get well?" Who would want to remain paralyzed? But some people want to stay in their current condition, even if it's not ideal. As C.S. Lewis wrote in *The Weight of Glory:*

> We are half-hearted creatures, fooling about with drink and sex and ambition when infinite joy is offered us, like an ignorant child who wants to go on making mud pies in a slum because he cannot imagine what is meant by the offer of a holiday at the sea. We are far too easily pleased.

We're comfortable with what we know, and new prospects can be scary, even if they're better. Like everyone else, ill people in Jesus's day made a life for themselves in spite of their infirmities. They had a spot where they could beg, probably had regular donors, and had an established routine. Getting well and providing for themselves would require work and lots of it. They would have to learn a trade and/or perform backbreaking labor for an established business. So no, not everyone would want to be made well.

Jesus's interaction with this man ended after He said, "Behold, you have become well; do not sin anymore, so that nothing worse happens to you" (John 5:14). The man was now on his own. He had to learn to live in the health that had been restored to him. Jesus did not give him money, new skills, or even establish an apprenticeship for him with a local successful merchant. Jesus's interest was the man's faith, and that's where His parting words focused.

Along those same lines, just as Jesus did not heal everyone, He also did not alleviate the financial burdens of the poor. His ministry was focused on economic prosperity, unlike so many that exist today. In fact, not one account is recorded of Jesus giving any money to help the poor. He fed, loved, prayed for, had compassion, and encouraged them, but He did not ease their financial burdens by providing them with wealth. Jesus wanted people's faith, not their wallets, to grow.

Thus, justice, by way of equity, was not something Jesus concerned Himself with. Instead, Jesus focused on equality—providing everyone with the opportunity to come to salvific faith through Him. In this way, He targeted the poor, sick, lowly, and downtrodden because "'it is not those who are healthy who need a physician, but those who are sick'" (Matthew 9:12b). The religious elite scorned, hated, and rejected Him. They thought their heavenly destinies were secure, clueless that they were rejecting the only Way to get there. Jesus rebuked them because of their arrogance and hypocrisy, not because they were wealthy oppressors victimizing the poor.

Jesus embodied true justice—exercising righteousness in every situation and relationship He was in. He made things right, not fair. And we should too.

Chapter Eight

Identity

Myth:

Jesus accepted people as they were and chose to be and didn't require them to change. We can be whoever we want and live however we want without fear of rejection from Jesus.

The Truth Within the Myth:

Our salvation doesn't depend on us—who we are, what we've done, or our current lifestyles.

Where Truth Gets Distorted by a Lie:

While Jesus accepts us as we are when we come to faith, He never leaves us as we are from that point on. We get a new identity—one that continually transforms more and more into His image. Once again, Satan wants to distort truth by turning our attention away from God and His holiness and toward ourselves and self-righteousness. If our perspective is,

"God wants me to be happy; so I can do whatever I want in pursuit of that happiness," we'll miss the mark every time. We'll never grow in our sanctification (if we're saved at all) because our focus is inward, not upward. However, if our perspective is, "'He must increase, but I must decrease'" (John 3:30), we'll be well on our way to living a Spirit-filled, spiritually transformed life.

A crucial step to embracing this perspective is understanding our identity, which we will now explore. We will first define it and unpack that definition. A lot more goes into our identities than we initially think, for we bear the image of the holy, incomprehensible God. We will then explore Jesus's identity and how ours is shaped by His example.

Defining Identity

Identity has been defined numerous ways by numerous people. The origin of our definitions matters. We are not at liberty to abide by worldly definitions alone, for we are not of this world. While identity is personal, it's not independent. God is the Author and sustainer of our lives, so we must recognize our dependence on Him when determining our identity and its definition. He is the Source, Architect, and Purpose of our identity. Any attempt to define it apart from Him is a fruitless, unsatisfying and, frankly, destructive endeavor. Thus, we will work from a theologically driven definition of identity as follows:

> *Identity is who God has created us to be for His glory, humanity's good, and for such a time as this.*

Who God Has Created Us to Be

In His Image

First and foremost, God created us in His image. Any study of identity must begin at the beginning: specifically, the creation account in Genesis. He spent the first five days of creation forming the universe and earth itself—light and darkness, the sky, atmosphere, land, plants, heavenly bodies, and then all the sea creatures and birds. Day six began with land animals. Then God turned His attention to the crown jewel of His creation: humanity. At this point, the narrative shifts from a succinct, descriptive account to an explanation. Before this, God hadn't revealed any reasoning behind His creations nor told us how He created them. Now, however, God explains…

> Then God said, "Let Us make man in Our image, according to Our likeness; and let them rule over the fish of the sea and over the birds of the sky and over the cattle and over all the earth, and over every creeping thing that creeps on the earth." God created man in His own image, in the image of God He created him; male and female He created them. (Genesis 1:26–27)

Notice what God says first: "Let Us make man in Our image." Unlike the rest of creation, humans were created to be like God, to share His some of His innate qualities and characteristics, and to experience relationship with Him distinct from everything else. What exactly are those innate qualities and characteristics? This is a bit more difficult to determine, since God never defines it explicitly in Scripture. However, through much study, prayer, and reflection on other passages in God's Word, we can learn quite a bit.

Theologians have wrestled with this concept for centuries, and they've found several plausible interpretations. Most have suggested that being created in God's image refers to the spiritual/immaterial aspect of our beings, since He is a Spirit and stands outside physical creation.[46] Augustine pursued that thought and added that the image includes human memory, intelligence, and will, because each of those components is necessary for knowing and loving God.[47] These views prioritize (seemingly exclusively) the unseen over the seen—the immaterial over the physical, and are widely accepted.

Other theories have arisen over the years. These go a bit further and suggest that the image of God (*imago Dei*) includes physical components as well. They suggest that God is not solely spiritual but has some kind of physical form that humanity is fashioned after. The main argument for this view comes from Genesis 5:3, which reads, "When Adam had lived one hundred and thirty years, he became the father of a son in his own likeness, according to his image, and named him Seth." The Hebrew terms used for "likeness" and "image" here are the same as those used in Genesis 1. Therefore, some have concluded that humanity resembles God in physical form as well.[48]

Another view considers image and likeness primarily in regard to relationship and suggests that "the relationship between male and female is in some way analogous to the relationship among the persons of the Trinity."[49] This view is supported by the reference to the Trinity in Genesis 1:26a: "Then God said, 'Let *Us* make man in *Our* image'" (emphasis added). This is one of the first glimpses we have into the Trinity, revealing that, while God is One God, He is three persons. God exists in perfect relationship and community with Himself. He's not solitary or lonely but is complete in and of Himself, embodying love, harmony, and communion. When He decided to create humanity in His image, He gave us the opportunity to know Him, as well as to live in relationship with Him.

Finally, another view interprets the image as a term of kind and kinship.[50] In the creation account, God created everything after its own kind—every plant and form of vegetation, every sea creature, bird, and land animal was created according to its own kind (or species). Sunflowers don't produce rose seeds, elephants don't birth monkeys, and eagles don't lay alligator eggs. While obvious differences arise when procreating (being fruitful and multiplying never meant producing exact replicas), each kind multiplies within its own species. To that end, some believe that being made in God's image means we are after His own kind. Just as Seth was born to Adam and Eve and bore their image and likeness, we were created by God to bear His.

An argument can be made for humanity's kinship to God as well.[51] We aren't made only according to His kind; we are also made as His sons and daughters. God as our Heavenly Father is a concept steeped in and expounded upon throughout Scripture. He refers to Israel as His son and firstborn (Exodus

4:22, Hosea 11:1). He punishes them "just as a man disciplines his son" (Deuteronomy 8:5). He is "a father of the fatherless," (Psalm 68:5), has compassion "just as a father has compassion on his children," (Psalm 103:13), is called "our Father," (Isaiah 63:16), demands honor as a Father (Malachi 1:6), and is known as our Father because He created us (Malachi 2:10). These Old Testament references are but a taste of what Jesus (and later the apostles) would teach us about God as our Heavenly Father.

During His earthly ministry, Jesus made it clear that He was God's Son. "All things have been handed over to Me by My Father; and no one knows the Son except the Father; nor does anyone know the Father except the Son, and anyone to whom the Son wills to reveal Him" (Matthew 11:27). Jesus became "flesh, and dwelt among us, and we saw His glory, glory as of the only begotten from the Father, full of grace and truth" (John 1:14). He did nothing of His own initiative, doing only what the Father wanted Him to do (John 5:19–32). He also made it clear that if we do not know Him (Jesus), we would never know His Father: "You know neither Me nor My Father; if you knew Me, you would know My Father also" (John 8:19b).

Sin broke the innate familial relationship between humanity and God, but Jesus made it possible for that relationship to be restored. God isn't just Israel's Father, nor only Jesus's. He's ours too, if we are saved. He calls us to live out our identity as His image bearers and children. We must glorify our "Father who is in heaven" (Matthew 5:16), we must be perfect, as our "heavenly Father is perfect" (Matthew 5:48), He gives us what is good because He's our Father (Matthew 7:11), we have "received a spirit of adoption as sons" (Romans 8:15), and we exist for Him because we came from Him (1 Corinthians 8:6). Every person bears the image of God, but only those who make Him Lord will live out His image effectively.

These last paragraphs have barely scratched the surface of this immense topic, but each view presents logical and doctrinally sound points regarding the *imago Dei*. We cannot fully exhaust this doctrine because Scripture never expounds on it, and we are finite beings, incapable of fully understanding our infinite Maker. We will also never fully be like God, because He is altogether distinct from every created being. But He did create us like Himself in many ways. A summary of these viewpoints follows:

> Being made in the image and likeness of God includes, but is not limited to our physical form, our immaterial disposition, including memory, intelligence, and will, our ability and purpose to have a relationship with both God and man, and being created according to God's kind and as His children in Christ.

Our identity, then, begins with understanding that we are made in God's image. We are not the product of some random cosmic accident, nor are we an afterthought God created on a whim. He created us intentionally to be like Him, to be with Him, and to live for Him in this world.

Male and Female

God is the source and architect of our identity. Bearing God's image means embracing His design. We've explored several aspects of His image and what they mean for humanity as a whole, but God made an important distinction among humanity that reflects his design for it— He created both males and females. Twenty years ago, we wouldn't have needed to address this point. But since gender is being viciously attacked in our world and culture today, it's prudent to probe it a bit. Satan uses it to wreak havoc on countless lives, so Christians must know and stand up for truth if we hope to defeat him.

As we've read, God created humanity in His own image. "Male and female He created them" (Genesis 1:27). Two genders. That's it. It's pretty straightforward and has been for thousands of years. Yet, today this truth is being compromised, deconstructed, and utterly rejected. Before writing this book, I thought such confusion was confined primarily to the west. However, gender- identity issues apparently plague numerous cultures all over the world. Now, shockingly, studies show that people have created more than eighty gender identities.[52]

Eighty.

When I was in college, I took a Bible class that was notorious for its difficulty. Students dreaded the infamous "Bible 350" class that would require countless hours of strenuous bookwork. One repeated assignment throughout the course was to glean as many facts from a passage as we could. Think

Sherlock Holmes. The professor gave us a passage and told us to write a minimum of twenty observations about it. It was difficult at first, but I loved it. Once you start looking, you start asking questions, and truth becomes a goldmine.

Today, instead of constructively studying truth and gleaning principles from it, people make up lies and destroy themselves with them. I do have to applaud their creativity in coming up with over eighty gender identities from the original (and sufficient) two. But I also cringe at the irony: people are exercising their God-given creativity to destroy His masterful creation. God created two beautiful, powerful works of art in gender with the potential to discover incomprehensible joy and purpose in Him.

But instead of embracing their perfectly crafted identities, humanity trashes, mutilates, and mocks them. We throw tantrums in our defiance and delude ourselves into thinking we're free. None of this should surprise us, since it's been happening for thousands of years:

> They did not honor Him as God or give thanks, but they became futile in their speculations, and their foolish heart was darkened...They exchanged the truth of God for a lie, and worshiped and served the creature rather than the Creator. (excerpts from Romans 1:21, 25).

The moment people turn away from God and try to find fulfillment apart from Him, the world suffers. It began with Adam and Eve and has continued ever since. As people turn away from God, they grow accustomed to darkness and forget how glorious and beautiful the Light is. Then we start craving darkness, attempting to fill an insatiable hole that only tunnels deeper into the depths of depravity. That's exactly what's happening with the transgender movement in our culture today. Men and women are boring holes deeper in the caverns of Satan's lies by rejecting their God-given genders and redefining them to whatever "feels right" in the moment. But scurrying away from light doesn't make it disappear. We can dig deep enough and close our eyes so we don't see it, but it still exists, and we fool ourselves, thinking it's not relevant.

God is clear about gender: there are only two. Nowhere does Scripture talk about or even hint at additional genders or alternative options to man and woman. Nowhere in Scripture is there a whisper about an individual being able to choose which gender he/she identifies as. Scripture talks about debase sexual behavior like homosexuality and extramarital affairs, but gender-identity issues aren't present. Some believe that, if the Bible doesn't condemn a specific behavior, they have the right to create new theological ground. "Well," they reason, "the Bible never says we have to remain our biological gender, so it must be okay for us to change it." That thought process is faulty on so many levels. It's hermeneutically irresponsible, a logical fallacy (argument from silence), and ultimately, heretical.

Here's an example for you. Kids are funny creatures. My husband and I have been blessed with four daughters, and the most surprising aspect of parenthood so far is how entertaining they are. We're constantly cackling over their silly antics, word choices, and theatrics. Their ability to think outside the box is fascinating because their boxes are still forming. Like any family, we have rules. One of these rules is that we're allowed to draw only on those thin, white sheets called paper. This rule didn't always exist because, well, it's common sense. Or so we thought. One day, while changing the sheets, I discovered that one of our daughters, who was six at the time (well into the "you know better than that!" age), decided to write her name accompanied by all kinds of drawings on the wall next to her bed. When confronted, she initially denied it but then said, "Well, you never told me I *couldn't* write on the wall!" True. But then we shouldn't have had to, or so the proceeding lecture went.

Scripture is silent on specific issues like transgenderism because it hadn't been "written on the wall" yet. Cross-dressing, alternative pronoun usage, "family friendly" drag shows, and genital mutation[53] wasn't how people demonstrated sexual sin when the Bible was written. However, the blanket rule regarding sexual purity covers many laws, narratives, and teachings throughout the Word. God's design for sexual purity is one man and one woman (both biological and self-identifying as such, respectively) becoming one flesh through sex within the lifelong covenant of marriage.[54] Any act, belief, or thought contradicting this is sin.

A whole lot of people have argued for a whole lot of years about specific gender issues under the blanket rule of sexual purity. However, at least four truths remain clear in Scripture[55]: there are only two gender options (male and female), gender and sex cannot be separated, we don't get to choose which we are, and God has a purpose for the gender He made us.

We've already noted that God created only two genders. However, the term "gender" is nearly as fluid as the term "love" nowadays, made even more confusing by liberals' attempts to redefine language to suit their purposes. Liberals have made a harsh distinction between sex and gender, suggesting sex is someone's physical characteristics assigned at birth, while gender is however someone wishes to identify apart from their biology:

> Unlike natal sex, gender is not made up of binary forms. Instead, gender is a broad spectrum. A person may identify at any point within this spectrum or outside of it entirely. People may identify with genders that are different from their natal sex or none at all. These identities may include transgender, nonbinary, or gender-neutral. There are many other ways in which a person may define their own gender.[56]

These claims have no basis in reality, science, or religion. But most importantly for the Christian, no division exists in Scripture either—gender and sex cannot be separated.

According to both God and science, we have no control over our gender; it's decided for us at the moment of conception. There are real cases of people struggling with gender identity, a diagnosis that was once referred to as "Gender Identity Disorder," but is now called "Gender Dysphoria" in an attempt to destigmatize people receiving this diagnosis.[57] And let me be clear: to struggle with gender dysphoria is not a sin any more than struggling with alcoholism or gluttony. We live in a broken world, and we each have different trials. To be tempted is not a sin. Remember, Jesus was tempted aggressively by Satan himself. But to act on and succumb to temptation resulting in disobedience to God is a sin. Struggling with inappropriate thoughts regarding your gender identity is not a sin, but taking action to transform those thoughts into reality is. When we do so, we act as our own god instead of submitting to the only true God and His plan for us. Christians struggling with gender dysphoria should seek counseling and therapy with the goal of submitting their thoughts and desires to God. They should not cave or embrace those impulses just because it's culturally acceptable.

Complicating this (and many other issues) is the silence heard from many pulpits today on the subject. Many members of the clergy today refuse to talk about cultural issues, or worse, they declare approval of behaviors directly contradicting Scripture. That's why it's crucial for each and every Christian to know Scripture so they can responsibly discern the truth within it. If, God forbid, we find ourselves under church leadership that defies God's Word and refuses to alter its course, we must seek membership elsewhere. If our church leadership remains silent, we must pray and respectfully encourage them to speak up. Regardless, we must mature in our faith enough to feed ourselves and discern the truth of Scripture.

Gender is assigned to us; we do not choose it for ourselves. Because of this, we must trust and remember that the "Gender Assigner" is also the Author and Sustainer of the universe, and He doesn't make mistakes. Countless young men and women are now hearing that they're unhappy because they were born the wrong gender. That's a lie created in the pit of hell, and it's one way Satan plants seeds of distrusting God. To believe God made a mistake in gender assignment is to believe numerous lies about Him—that He's not omnipotent, that He doesn't love you, that He doesn't know what's best for you, and that He could make a mistake. Most people don't realize they believe this, and that's the way Satan wants it. Again, within every lie is some truth. In this case, the truth is that the person is genuinely unhappy. The lie is the explanation that his or her unhappiness stems from being the "wrong" gender. If Satan can grip someone with that thought and encourage them to take action, he can cause (and has caused) irreparable harm.

People of all ages and genders are rapidly pursuing hormonal and surgical intervention to transition themselves from one gender to the other. While not all transition interventions bear permanent ramifications, the longer and more involved the interventions, the more irreversible they become. In 2021, nearly 1,400 minors ages six to seventeen started taking puberty blockers, and over 4,000 were treated with hormone therapy (hormone treatments that mimic puberty for the opposite gender of the patient).[58] For ages thirteen to seventeen in the same year, 282 girls underwent mastectomies—the removal of perfectly healthy breasts of teenage girls.[59] And the numbers are only growing.

If used for a significant length of time, these drastic treatments and surgeries can have lifelong ramifications. This begs the question: why are they allowed to do it in the first place? In our country, minors aren't allowed to vote, rent cars or apartments, check into hotels, buy or drink alcohol, or serve in the military.

Most of these restrictions are because minors aren't deemed responsible enough (or "of age") to do so. If that's true, why does anyone think minors are mature enough to make life-altering decisions about their gender and treatments thereof?

Further, many who do undergo treatment for gender change regret it later. Countless stories exist of people who thought transitioning would solve all their problems, only to realize it made them worse. The transgender community that once embraced them with open arms regarding their "freedom of choice" disavow them if they change their minds. Indeed, those who de-transition experience "online vitriol, doxing, harassment and death threats after they made the tough decisions to exit what they describe as inward-looking and even 'cult-like' trans groups."[60] Rejected by the community they once viewed as savior-like, they're abandoned because their experience runs contrary to the group's narrative.

Fortunately, God never leaves them, and the church is learning how to embrace de-transitioners in ways that help them heal and (re)establish their identity in Christ. God provides redemption and healing for all who turn to Him, and peace can be found regardless of past decisions. However, some physical consequences are impossible to eradicate. Some gender transitioning procedures are irreversible. One cannot go back in time and have natural breasts again after a mastectomy. Bottom surgery procedures have even more dire complications.

The transgender agenda, especially for minors, isn't just irresponsible. It's evil. It's child abuse. And it's the result of people, particularly Christians, sitting idly and silently on the sidelines as it ravages our culture. "Letting people make their own choices" and "staying in our own lane" isn't an option if we're to save future generations (children!) from permanent mutilation of their bodies and deep scars in their minds and hormones. Silence leads to unadulterated evil.

We must speak, and our words must declare God's truth in love: He is all-powerful. He does love us, more than we'll ever realize. He does know what's best for us, and He never has and never will make a mistake. God has a plan for us as the gender He created us, and the only way to receive true joy and contentment is by embracing the design He authored from the foundations of the world. Christians cannot believe otherwise, nor can we encourage others to do so by remaining silent on this issue.

Gender is a significant part of our identity, but it's not the only part. Not by a long shot. We were created in His image as men and women to fulfill a purpose with eternal ramifications.

For His Glory

God is both the Source and Architect of our identity. He crafted us in His image and in one of two categories—male or female. Yet His masterpiece of humanity was never meant to sit on a proverbial shelf to be admired. He created us for a purpose, and we must understand that purpose before we can understand our identity.

The primary purpose of our lives, as previously discussed throughout this volume, is to bring glory to God and enjoy Him in the process.[61] As stated in our chapter on suffering,

God is glorified when we, His children and created beings, choose to love, serve, and obey Him. Glorifying Him means to ascribe Him honor, worth, and praise. It means to worship and exalt Him—to put Him in His rightful place in our lives as Lord, Savior, and King. It means to be His image-bearers and to represent Him to the world for the purpose of redemption through the gospel of Jesus Christ.

Glorifying God isn't just a part of our identity; it's our identity's purpose.

The purpose of our lives is determined by whatever we worship. Said another way, what we worship becomes our purpose. If we worship God, we strive to bring Him glory in every aspect of our lives, thus fulfilling our purpose. If we worship anything else, our purpose becomes worthless. We spend our lives chasing after things that don't matter and bear no positive eternal significance.

Objects of our worship range far and wide. Some worship vintage cars; others worship their shoe collection. To probe a bit deeper, some worship busyness, incapable of being content or feeling fulfilled unless their calendars are full and without lull. Others worship money and spend their lives increasing their net worth at any cost. Some worship image and a select group of people's opinion about them. Others worship rebellion, advocating causes that polarize people for the sake of upheaval. Some worship their families and have no life outside them. Others worship travel and experiences. Some worship success and define it in numerous ways. Others worship health and obsess over dieting and exercise.

Regardless of the object of our worship, if it's not God, we've missed the mark and therefore miss the purpose of our lives. And that's a huge reason people struggle so much today. Depression, anxiety, gender dysphoria, addictions, apathy, rebellion…all these and more stem from misaligned objects of our worship. We don't fulfill the purpose we were created for, and understandably, we suffer because of it.

I had this conversation with our daughters the other day. We were talking about Jesus being the Head of the body of Christ, and what that looks like for us as members of that body (how we can fulfill our purpose as Christians). I looked at my coffee mug perched on my desk and asked them to imagine that our roles were as fingers in the body of Christ. The head (specifically, *my* head) wants to pick up that cup and drink a sip of coffee so it can absorb some much-desired caffeine. But what if my fingers didn't want to comply? What if they thought holding a coffee mug was beneath them, so they started jerking around every which way and spilling the coffee all over the desk and on themselves, getting burned in the process? Not only would I not get the caffeine I want, but now I'd have to clean up a huge mess. While this is arguably a silly illustration, the point is that, when we reject God and His purpose for lives, we wreak havoc and end up harming ourselves and others.

We were created to glorify God—to stand in awe of Him and ascribe Him praise, honor, and utmost worth in every aspect of our lives. His glory is intrinsic to our identity, and trying to fill that with anything else leaves us unsettled, ill-content, and longing for more.

For Humanity's Good

The source and architect of our identity is God, and our primary purpose is to glorify and enjoy Him forever. But we cannot fulfill our purpose in a silo. We were not created in a vacuum, and we don't live in one now. God created human beings to be relational (male and female is evidence of that in itself). We can't accomplish much of anything of worth without the involvement of other people. Inventions, discoveries, noteworthy works of literature, architecture, medical advances, and companies, while often attributed to one person as the source, could not exist without the involvement of others as they progressed. Further, one cannot receive inspiration ex nihilo (out of nothing) either. Even if people don't inspire us to accomplish something, other aspects of creation do, and this expresses the Creator. While some of us are more hermit-like than others, the fact remains that we were created to be relational. Without other people, we can't live out our identity as God designed it.

But it's not enough merely to realize or acquiesce to the relational aspect of our identity. In our pursuit of glorifying God, we must embrace and then prioritize the good of others as well. Innate within each of us is a desire to make the world a better place somehow, bettering it for the sake of ourselves, families, and fellow man. The vast majority of disagreements between liberals and conservatives are simply a matter of how to do so. No one (except extremists bent on accomplishing demonic purposes, I suppose) actually desires the demise of others. But strong opinions lie on both sides as liberals and conservatives debate what betterment looks like and how we should accomplish it.

For Christians, desiring the betterment of our society and world is the result of first loving God, then loving others. Indeed, Jesus repeated the most important commandments:

> "You shall love the Lord your God with all your heart, and with all your soul, and with all your mind." This is the great and foremost commandment. The second is like it, "You shall love your neighbor as yourself." On these two commandments depend the whole Law and the Prophets. (Matthew 22:37–40)

Loving God is a crucial step to glorifying Him and living out our identity. Loving others shares that goal. If you recall, loving someone is *purposefully, consistently, and sacrificially seeking their good as defined by God and purposed for His glory.* When we love others in accordance with truth, we glorify God and thereby fulfill our identity as His image-bearers on earth. The crux of the issue, then, is loving others in a way that prioritizes their good as God defines it.

We do not need to rehash all the examples of how to do this, but we must remember to disregard any opinion, policy, political initiative, or educational or church teaching that contradicts Scripture. The terrifying part of our current cultural climate isn't that evil policies exist. We live in a broken world, after all. The problem is the number of self-proclaimed Christians who advocate them. Abortion and transgender policies alone should be enough to cause Christians to run from the political party that promotes them. Instead, some Christians weigh the options, and while perhaps agreeing that those issues are bad, they're apparently not bad enough to keep these people from voting for candidates from that party. Further, some self-professed Christians even advocate that issues like abortion and transgenderism aren't bad at all. This glaringly contradicts Scripture. One simply cannot be a genuine follower of Jesus and advocate foundational tenets He stood against.

For Such a Time As This

This brings us to a vital point in any discussion of identity: the general identity of humanity as image-bearers of God versus the specific identity of people who are saved by grace through faith in Jesus. All humans are in the first category. Every person who's ever lived was created as an image-bearer of God, distinct from the rest of creation. We are not the evolutionary product of monkeys any more than we just magically appeared with the rest of the universe from a singularly random "big bang." We are the crown jewel of God's creation, the only part of His created order that bears His image and that He wants an eternal relationship with.

Only one kind of relationship with God is inherent within humanity post fall, though—that of wrath, damnation, and separation. Again, as sinners, all we deserve is to rot in hell for eternity. Yet (and what a beautiful word that is!), God intervened. He sovereignly orchestrated a gospel narrative so powerful, it literally plucks people out of the depths of hell and raises them to life in Christ. By way of reminder, the gospel is:

> The good news of God's plan to rescue a spiritually
> dead, broken, condemned, and sin-enslaved world,

offering forgiveness of sin, eternal life, and the restoration of peace with Him through the comprehensive and final sacrifice of Jesus Christ— who was born of a virgin, lived a sinless life, died on the cross, was buried, and rose again—bringing us to life in Him, adopting us into His family, and securing us in His glorious future.

This is what's available to those who repent of their sins and call on the name of Jesus in faith. It awaits those who make Christ Lord of their lives and submit to His leadership in every aspect of them. Those who do so are moved from the general image-bearing group into the special, life-transforming group of those who follow Christ with utmost devotion.

The timing of our salvation and subsequent sanctification is no accident. God created us for such a time as this so we can be His hands, feet, voice, and heart to the world and so we may lead others to faith in Christ as well. This is a vital part of our special identity as disciples of Christ. We can't ignore it if we want to succeed in living out our purpose.

That phrase, "for such a time as this" was borrowed from Mordecai's famous words to Esther, when he implored her to risk her life on behalf of their people, Israel:

> "For if you remain silent at this time, relief and deliverance will arise for the Jews from another place and you and your father's house will perish. And who knows whether you have not attained royalty for such a time as this?" (Esther 4:14)

Esther had won the beauty contest of a hundred lifetimes and became the queen to King Ahasuerus, who, at the time, "reigned from India to Ethiopia over 127 provinces" (Esther 1:1). Unbeknownst to King Ahasuerus, Esther was a Jew, and his top advisor, Haman, received his permission to kill all the Jews because of a personal vendetta he had against Mordecai, Esther's cousin. To thwart Haman's evil plan, Esther needed to talk to the king. But this would mean risking her life, because to approach the king without being summoned would result in death unless he held out his golden scepter. She was understandably afraid. Yet Mordecai's famous challenge put things in perspective. What if the reason she became queen in the first place was to speak up and save the Jews?

Turns out, it was.

She approached the king, despite having zero confidence he'd accept her. Through a series of events, she gained his favor, discredited Haman, and saved her people.

Part of our identity, like Esther's, is the time in which we live. We may never have the kingdom-sized platform Esther had. However, God placed us in a specific place at a specific time in history for a reason. Our sphere of influence could be as small as our immediate family, or as large as millions of followers on social media and other platforms. No matter how many people are within the scope of our influence, we must consistently ask ourselves, "Do I influence them toward Christ or away from Him? Do I inspire their faith to grow, or am I an obstacle that hinders it?"

My husband and I had an interesting first date. I lovingly refer to it as an interrogation, because I spent over three hours at Starbucks, grilling him with the biggest, most potent "red flag" issues I could think of. One of the very first questions I asked him was, "What do you want written on your tombstone?" Needless to say, I wasn't at a point in my life where I wanted to waste time on a relationship headed nowhere. Turns out, he wasn't either. So we conversed. He answered my questions and then started shooting them right back (in a charming, good-natured way, of course). We were honest from the start and tackled major points of potential tension on that first date: faith, denominational backgrounds, politics, money, kids, family issues, faith heritage, etc.

Aside from personally thinking this is the best way to begin any dating relationship, I share this with the intent of encouraging you to be honest with yourself. Look at your life from a helicopter point of view. Where do you live? Who makes up your circles (inner, middle, and outer)? Where do you work? What issues currently threaten the advancement of the gospel in your context? What issues do you need to repent of and deal with personally so Christ is seen more clearly in you?

Just as we were not created as a mistake, we were not placed in our specific contexts by mistake either. God wants to use you exactly where you are to make an eternal impact for His kingdom. He is the Source and Architect of our identity. He also provides us with our purpose: to bring glory to Him and lift others up through the gospel of Jesus Christ for such a time as this.

Jesus's Identity and Ours

As with everything else in our life and faith, Jesus is the perfect and ultimate example for us regarding identity. We differ from Him in obvious ways, of course, since He was God incarnate. But by observing key aspects of His life and ministry, we can better understand His identity and how He lived it out according to His Father's purposes.

Just as God created us with intention, Jesus came to earth in a deliberate way, place, and time in history. He entered the world the same way we do: as a baby. The Holy Spirit caused the virgin Mary to be with child, the manner and significance of which has been intensely debated for centuries.[62] The point worth highlighting here, however, is that He was supernaturally conceived, and He grew exactly the same way every other human baby has before and after Him. He could've come any way He pleased—as an adult, as an adolescent born into a royal family, as a young man ready to begin His earthly ministry. He could've come on chariots of fire in spectacular fashion, causing everyone's jaws to drop and gathering an enormous following from the get-go. But He didn't. He came humbly and within the order of creation He'd established long ago.[63]

Unlike us, Jesus chose when and how He would enter the world. He chose to be born, like every other human, and interestingly, He chose to be born into a family without abounding financial means. The King of the Universe, who owned everything, gave it all up and was born owning nothing. His family didn't have much, either. While Joseph was a carpenter, the Gospel of Luke records that Mary and Joseph offered "a pair of turtledoves or two young pigeons" when they presented Jesus to the Lord (Luke

2:24). This kind of offering, "which was prescribed for Israelites of humble means and thus identifies Mary and Joseph with the lower economic classes in Palestine, was prescribed for the purification of the birth mother."[64]

Jesus grew up without a lot of material wealth and maintained that status into His ministry, as we gather with clues like this, when Jesus said, "The foxes have holes and the birds of the air have nests, but the Son of Man has nowhere to lay His head" (Matthew 8:20). He also sent His disciples on missions without monetary security, trusting that God would provide them everything they would need (Matthew 10:5–15).

Even though Jesus possessed everything by right, He forfeited material comforts, political status, and economic success to prioritize His Father's purposes. He didn't find His identity in trivial, superficial matters. His purpose was to usher in God's kingdom on earth through the gospel for God's glory and humanity's ultimate good, for such a time as this.

While hesitant to shout His identity from the rooftops in many cases, Jesus did reveal who He was throughout His ministry. He made several metaphorical statements, some of which we will briefly observe, both to learn more about Him and to understand our identity better as His followers.

Light of the World

> "I am the Light of the world; he who follows Me will not walk in the darkness, but will have the Light of life" (John 8:12).

Light and darkness representing God and sin respectively is found throughout Scripture. In the Old Testament, David writes, "The Lord is my light and my salvation" (Psalm 27:1a). In the New Testament, we read that God is light (1 John 1:5). He opens our eyes and hearts to truth and allows us to embrace it as we leave behind the darkness of our sin. Light is also linked to both God's Word (how we get to know God) and righteousness (how we act once we've encountered it).[65] It's fitting, thus, that Jesus, the Word made flesh, identified as the Light of the World. "In Him was life, and the life was the Light of men" (John 1:4).

Part of Jesus's identity was to usher light into a dark world. Like turning on headlights in the dead of night, His coming shattered the darkness the world was accustomed to. His light made a lot of people uncomfortable (and still does), so many refuse to accept Him. But those who do accept Him allow their eyes to adjust slowly to His glory and the joyful, full life offered them.

Because we're created in His image, it's no surprise that aspects of Jesus's identity are ours to embrace personally as well. Jesus told His disciples,

> "You are the light of the world. A city set on a hill cannot be hidden; nor does anyone light a lamp and put it under a basket, but on the lampstand, and it gives light to all who are in the house. Let your light shine before men in such a way that they may see your good works, and glorify your Father who is in heaven." (Matthew 5:14–16)

217

Bearing His name also means bearing His light and shining it for all to see. Indeed, "if we say that we have fellowship with Him and yet walk in the darkness, we lie and do not practice the truth" (1 John 1:6). We cannot call ourselves Christians if we don't embrace His light and emulate it in our own lives. Part of Christ's identity is shining His light and opening people's eyes and hearts to the truth of the gospel. If we're His, we'll do the same.

Bread of Life

> "I am the bread of life; he who comes to Me will not hunger, and he who believes in Me will never thirst." (John 6:35)

As mentioned previously, I struggled with an eating disorder for several years in college. Eating disorders are an addiction of sorts. I was addicted to trying to control at least one area of my life (which could be another book in itself). It started as a diet. My goal was to lose twelve pounds. When those twelve pounds went away, I still wasn't content with what I saw in the mirror, so I told myself I should lose five more. Then another five, and another. And so it went until I stopped weighing myself, though I had dropped well into the eighty-pound range.

As you can imagine, I wasn't in a good place. I had deprived my body of nutrition for months on end, and this took a serious toll. I had trouble focusing, was super emotional, my hormones were completely out of whack, and I developed insomnia. I was beyond exhausted all the time. I ran on fumes until I went on a missions trip after graduating college. While there, I fell ill and landed in the hospital, being told I would die within six weeks without medical intervention.

I was a mess.

There are major consequences for not adequately nourishing your body. I know that better than most, and it took years to get back to a healthy place. Just the same, there are dire consequences for neglecting to nourish our souls. Jesus knew that better than anyone, which is why He provided us with the metaphor of being the "bread of life."

If you remember from chapter 3, Satan tried to tempt Jesus with bread, saying, "If You are the Son of God, command that these stones become bread."[66] Jesus could have done so instantly, but He wasn't about to acquiesce Satan. Instead, He replied with Scripture, stating, "It is written, 'Man shall not live on bread alone, but on every word that proceeds out of the mouth of God.'"[67] Jesus chose to feed Himself truth instead of physical bread. We need bread for our physical bodies to survive, but we need truth for our souls to live.

Jesus encouraged His followers to do the same. He said, "Do not work for the food which perishes, but for the food which endures to eternal life; which the Son of Man will give to you."[68] Our souls need truth. We crave it, and we can get it only through Jesus, the truth incarnate: "The Word became flesh and dwelt among us."[69] By claiming to be the "bread of life," Jesus confirmed His identity as truth, saying that we have to consume Him—read about, study, meditate upon, memorize, and prioritize a relationship with Him if we want to experience eternal life.

If Jesus is the bread of life, Christians are the bakery employees. God provides the bread, and we are tasked with distributing it. We absolutely should meet the physical needs of those around us, but not to the extent that we neglect to meet their spiritual needs as well. Our identity is inextricably linked with Christ's. As we partake of His bread, we share it with others so they can do the same.

The Vine and the Branches

> "I am the true vine, and My Father is the vinedresser. Every branch in Me that does not bear fruit, He takes away; and every branch that bears fruit, He prunes it so that it may bear more fruit...Abide in Me, and I in you. As the branch cannot bear fruit of itself unless it abides in the vine, so neither can you unless you abide in Me." (John 15:1–2,4)

We have a lot of beautiful oak trees in our yard. In fact, this is one of my favorite spots in late autumn because when the leaves change, our yard explodes with color—red, orange, and yellow. There are many benefits to having aged trees in our yard, but there are also a few drawbacks...like fallen branches. Every year, we lose branches. Most are relatively small, but some are so big they'd do major damage if they fell on something other than the ground.

I love this metaphor of Jesus as the vine because it reminds me of His strength and how much we depend on Him to survive and thrive. Jesus is the ultimate vine—immune to disease, decay, and other such inconveniences. His perfection is our respite. His vigor is our lifeline. His Father, the vinedresser, placed Him exactly where He wanted Him in history, to usher in the gospel and give life to those who accept Him. Christ's identity is secure, based on His Father's will. This makes possible the sweet, perfect, and completely satisfactory relationship between the two.

Jesus graciously extends us an invitation to join their relationship as branches, according to this metaphor. We are grafted in, so to speak, and the proof of our connection is the fruit we bear. If we don't bear fruit, like the dead branches in our yard, we're useless and the vinedresser will break us off and discard us. In case that doesn't sound so bad, let's remember that discarded branches await no other fate than hell: "If anyone does not abide in Me, he is thrown away as a branch and dries up; and they gather them, and cast them into the fire and they are burned" (John 15:6).

Hardly a more unpleasant topic exists than that of hell, but its unpopularity doesn't eradicate its reality. While we were all created in God's image, only those who don't forfeit their identities to the enemy can become His in Jesus. Autonomy is a dangerous mirage in the realm of faith, and those who fall into its trap will scarcely find a way out. If we do not submit to Christ's lordship, we submit to Satan's by default. Our identities and eternities are secured in only one of two places: the Vine of Christ or the burning pit of Satan. We all find ourselves defaulting to Satan because of our sin. Blessed are those who receive God's pardon through Christ and wear its cloak intentionally all their days!

Back to our current metaphor. Notice the tense of the vine/branch relationship: it's constant. It's not enough for a branch to merely be connected to the vine, because superficial connection does not bear fruit and runs the risk of being broken off. We're charged to abide actively in Christ, to embrace Him continuously every day, and to allow the truth that flows through His veins to infuse life into ours as well. To be a Christian is to receive and then live out our new lives and identities in Him. Passiveness acts as a weight thrown around our branch, trying to break it off. Don't let it, friend. Actively pursue Jesus, for He is our lifeline, daily and for eternity. Our identity cannot be separated from His, for if we truly are His, we will bear the fruit He's predestined us to produce.

The Good Shepherd

> "I am the good shepherd; the good shepherd lays down His life for the sheep...I am the good shepherd, and I know My own and My own know Me." (John 10:11, 14)

I am far from an expert on sheep. Anything I know of the species I learned from Bible studies, since it's not exactly a thriving industry in southern California, where I grew up. Be that as it may, shepherding was a big deal in biblical times. We should do our best to understand it, especially because it was one way Jesus identified Himself.

One of the best examples of a shepherd in the Old Testament is David, who shepherded before becoming a soldier, and ultimately, the second king of Israel. As with most everything else he did, David was an excellent shepherd. He cared deeply for the sheep under his charge. Reflecting on his prior duties, he informed King Saul,

> "Your servant was tending his father's sheep. When a lion or a bear came and took a lamb from the flock, I went out after him and attacked him, and rescued it from his mouth; and when he rose up against me, I seized him by his beard and struck him and killed him. Your servant has killed both the lion and the bear." (1 Samuel 17:34–36a)

While I'd like to say I'd do the same, that wouldn't be remotely honest. If a bear wanted to snack on a sheep under my charge, I'd say, "Enjoy your meal." Then I'd scurry away and try my best to keep the others safe. Fortunately, that's not how David or Jesus approached shepherding. Each sheep was valuable; each was worth risking it all.

Jesus is the ultimate good shepherd, for He didn't merely risk His life. He willingly laid it down for His sheep. No sheep can save itself. Not from being lost, and certainly not from the threat of a hungry lion or bear. Just the same, we cannot save ourselves from sin, and we're no match for our "adversary, the devil, [who] prowls around like a roaring lion, seeking someone to devour."[70] We "were considered as sheep to be slaughtered," but fortunately, Christ intervened.[71] He gave us life by laying His down; He protected us by going to the cross. By doing so, He makes us a secure and eternal part of His family.

His affection toward us did not cease on the cross, however. He still loves and protects us today by interceding for us in heaven.[72] He still is our Good Shepherd.

I love what Spurgeon wrote about Jesus's current prayers for us:

> We little know what we owe to our Savior's prayers. When we reach the hilltops of heaven and look back upon all the way whereby the Lord our God has led us, how we shall praise Him who, before the eternal throne, undid the mischief that Satan was doing upon the earth. How we shall thank Him because He never held His peace but day and night pointed to the wounds upon His hands and carried our names upon His breastplate![73]

If Christ is our shepherd, we are tasked with knowing and obeying His voice. Just as a sheep recognizes and follows the voice of its shepherd, we too must grow in our relationships with Christ so we may do the same. If we don't, we aren't His. We don't belong to His flock. Contrary to what many would like to believe, we are not at liberty to choose the parts of Jesus we like and discard others. If a sheep listens to his shepherd only when it's convenient for him, he'll end up in a heap of trouble. Just the same, when we follow only the things we like about Christ and His Word, we put ourselves at risk. Genuine believers genuinely believe. It's all or nothing. We either follow Christ or get led astray.

Way, the Truth, and the Life

> "I am the way, and the truth, and the life; no one comes to the Father but through Me." (John 14:6)

This one is more straight fact than metaphor, and it steps on a lot of cultural toes. The world has always wanted to find other ways to get to heaven (or find nirvana, attain utopia, or whatever end goal seems best at a given time). Declaring that there's only *one* way to get to heaven is not inclusive, not accepting of everyone, and just plain mean, according to some. Culture also screams that there's no such thing as objective truth. We've already seen this is a self-defeating statement. Making such a claim assumes the speaker knows at least one truth objectively. Finally, according to culture, life is what you make it. We should be free to live however we want, do whatever we want, and nowadays, be praised for our decisions.

Yet Jesus is clear as day about the topic: there is one way to heaven, objective truth exists, and life with Him is the only one worth living.

Jesus said,

> "Enter through the narrow gate; for the gate is wide and the way is broad that leads to destruction, and there are many who enter through it. For the gate is small and the way is narrow that leads to life, and there are few who find it." (Matthew 7:13–14)

He is the narrow gate. Even though He loves the world and offers salvation to everyone, He knows that many will reject Him. The majority will stick with what's easy and comfortable, disregarding truth and completely missing out on a thriving life in Him. Jesus did not come to make us comfortable; He came to make us courageous. He doesn't want us compliant with the world; He wants us competent and confident in Him. The exclusivity of Jesus and His offer of salvation are core attributes of His identity.

How does His exclusivity affect our identity? First, we become His only when we enter by way of the narrow gate of salvation through Him. Then, part of our purpose becomes extending His truth to everyone around us, regardless of the consequences to our comfort. It is easy to go with the world. It's easy just to go with the flow, let people do what they want, maintain the status quo, and refrain from creating waves. For a Christian, this behavior is cowardly and shameful. Obviously, the manner and timing of speaking truth matters. It's hardly appropriate to scream Bible verses at the top of our lungs during a board meeting or whack people over the heads with Bibles on the street. However, if we belong to Jesus, we must speak truth. We're not loving others if we don't.

Florida had an abnormally late-season hurricane last year, and our family knew several victims of its destruction. One family decided to stay, and during the storm noticed the lights were on in their next-door neighbor's house. This was odd, because the house belonged to an elderly woman who was supposed to have left for a shelter days before. The family kayaked over and found the poor woman shivering on top of her washing machine as water rose all around her. At first she was too terrified to move, but they gently coaxed the woman into their kayak and then paddled back to their house to safety.

Why do I share this story? Because the world is like that woman, and we are to be like the rescuing family. That woman had one chance to be rescued—one and only one way out. No one else knew where she was, and she couldn't call for help. The neighbors were her "only path to salvation," so to speak, and they ended up saving her life. She was understandably scared, but she got it together enough to recognize salvation when she saw it. As Christians, we have the way of salvation: Jesus Christ. Refusing to tell others about Him would be like those neighbors seeing the lights on in her house and saying, "Well, she chose to stay; she must know what she's doing." Or, when she initially rejected their offer due to fear, it would be like leaving and saying, "She made her choice." Ridiculous. But that's what we do on an eternal scale when we sit idly by and allow the world to drown in Satan's lies. It's not hateful to say there's only one way out and offer it. It's proof of your love for them and obedience to Christ.

Answering the "Why?"

Identity is like an iceberg, and we've glanced at only what's visible above the surface. God provides us with many more metaphors and instructions in His Word, showing us who we are and how we should go about our lives as His people.[74] We've touched upon the "who," "what," "when," "where" and "how" of identity, but we cannot conclude this topic without answering why. Why does it matter? Why does understanding and living out our identity in Christ matter so much?

It matters because, if we do not understand who we are in Christ, we'll never experience life the way He intended. For example, if we don't understand that we're free in Christ, we can't "lay aside every encumbrance and the sin which so easily entangles us" (Hebrews 12:1). We'll remain stuck in our sin, and like Israel of the Old Testament, we'll continue to make the same mistakes over and over and over again.

And consider eternal security. So many people have doubts regarding their salvation. "I said the prayer, but did it count? Did I miss something? Should I have said it a different way?" and on and on it goes. But when they realize that their identity is secure and untouchable in Jesus, that they can know for certain they have eternal life (1 John 5:13), they experience deep relief and peace in their minds.

The Christian life is not just about living with good morals. It's not just about gaining our "get out of hell free" card to cash in when we stand before Jesus one day. It's not just a resume bullet point that makes us feel better about ourselves and makes us look good in certain circles. Being a Christian is embracing the gospel of Jesus with every fiber of our being, living out the transforming power of the Holy Spirit fueled by our devotion to God's Word, and doing it all for God's glory. We cannot grow as Christians if we don't first know what being a Christian means. That's why identity is so important. We can't live out truth if we don't know it, just as we can't exercise a muscle we don't even know we have.

God created us in His image, as male or female, for the purpose of bringing Him glory on earth. As we pursue this goal, we will inevitably contribute to humanity's good, because we live in the exact times, places, and locations He predestined for us. We belong to Jesus if we believe and embrace His gospel. Then we spend the rest of our lives living out our identities as a new creations.

Jesus exuded our definition of identity perfectly as only He can:

> *Identity is who God has created us to be for His glory, humanity's good, and for such a time as this.*

We, as Christians, have the opportunity to follow in His footsteps. Our identity is inextricably linked with Jesus's, and the more we understand who He is, the more we'll understand our role in this life. But we accomplish this only when we keep Him in His rightful context—taking Him at His word and digging deep with proper hermeneutics to understand who He really is.

Concluding Thoughts

We've covered quite a bit of ground in this modest volume, and I pray it's been beneficial in your journey of becoming more like Jesus. Our time together began by identifying a historic issue that's plagued our current world perversely: Christians are taking Scripture, and particularly Jesus, out of context. We're guilty of being poor archeologists of God's Word, refusing to dig deep into its pages and glean truths to apply to our lives as His disciples. Instead, we pick and choose what we like, apply it if it's convenient, and thereby grossly transform Jesus into a fluffy, mild, soft, cuddly character who lacks substance. This is eons removed from the true Jesus of Scripture.

After identifying this issue, we equipped ourselves for the fight by defining terms. We defined basic but often controversially defined terms like the Bible, hermeneutics, truth, Christian, liberal, and conservative. Defining terms is crucial for understanding the rest of this volume and ensures we are on the same page as we proceed.

Chapter three introduced one of the biggest complications in taking Jesus out of context: that within every plausible lie or misunderstanding is at least a small measure of truth. Satan is the master of deception and the primary agent behind the movement of taking Jesus out of context. He derives his power by his cunning ability to weave just enough truth within a lie that it's easier to believe, and therefore, easier to disregard the truth we're supposed to uphold. We explored two main Scripture texts demonstrating this: the temptation and failure of Adam and Eve, and then the temptation and success of Jesus in the wilderness. Both of these accounts reveal Satan's crafty brilliance. They also show that the only way we can defeat him is by keeping Jesus and the truth of God's Word in their rightful contexts.

From that point on, we addressed specific topics about Jesus currently being attacked in our culture: judgment, love, suffering, justice, and identity. For each of these, we presented a present-day cultural myth—a lie that people believe about the topic in association with Christ. We then gleaned the truth within the myths and discussed in depth where and how the truth got distorted by lies. These topics are immense and our discussion of each was hardly conclusive, but we discovered how Jesus has been taken out of context. Then we put Him back in His rightful place as Scripture prescribes.

If you remember only one thought from this book, my prayer is that it's this: pursue Jesus in the context of Scripture. He is the only way to salvation, the only way to experience true life. Our decision about Him is the single most important one we will make in our lifetimes. Make it with eyes wide open, mind informed, and heart receptive to the gracious truth found only in Him.

This unrivaled tutor [Jesus] used as His class-book *the best of books.* Although able to reveal fresh truth, He preferred to expound the old…The readiest way to be spiritually rich in heavenly knowledge is to dig in this mine of diamonds, to gather pearls from this heavenly sea. When Jesus Himself sought to enrich others, He mined the quarry of Holy Scripture.[75]

Bibliography

Baucham, Voddie Jr. *Fault Lines.* Washington D.C.: Salem Books, 2021.

Carson, D.A. *The Gospel According to John.* Grand Rapids, MI: Wm. B. Eerdmans Publishing Company, 1991.

Erickson, Millard J. *Christian Theology (Second Edition).* Grand Rapids, Michigan: Baker Academic, 2007.

Jones, Beth Felker, and Jeffrey W. Barbeau. *The Image of God in an Image Driven Age: Explorations in Theological Anthropology.* Downers Grove, Illinois: InterVarsity Press, 2016.

Lloyd-Jones, D. Martyn. *Studies in the Sermon on the Mount.* Grand Rapids, Michigan: Wm. B. Eerdmans Publishing Company, 1976.

Spurgeon, Charles H. *Morning and Evening.* Edited by Alistair Begg. Wheaton, Illinois: Crossway, 2003.

Tozer, A.W. *The Knowledge of the Holy.* San Francisco, CA: HarperSanFrancisco, 1961.

Notes

[1] Llyod-Jones, D. Martyn. *Studies in the Sermon on the Mount.* Grand Rapids, Michigan: Wm. B. Eerdmans Publishing Company, 1976. p. 427.

[2] The only discrepancies found in the copies of Scripture we have today are grammatical and textual in nature. Some ancient manuscripts miss a word or add a phrase (translations we have today use brackets to indicate disputed words/phrases). But none of these bear any theological significance, and there aren't even enough of these textual discrepancies to fill a single piece of paper. God has preserved His Word supernaturally for centuries; it is absolutely worthy of our trust.

[3] Furby, Mindi Jo. *More than Words.* Bluffton, SC: KingsWynd Books, 2013. p. 87.

[4] https://ed.ted.com/lessons/jonathan-haidt-on-the-moral-roots-of-liberals-and-conversatives.

[5] *George Whitefield (1772). "The Works of the Reverend George Whitefield, M.A...: Containing All His Sermons and Tracts which Have Been Already Published: with a Select Collection of Letters... Also, Some Other Pieces on Important Subjects, Never Before Printed; Prepared by Himself for the Press; to which is Prefixed, an Account of His Life, Compiled from His Original Papers and Letters," p.27.*

[6] *George Whitefield (1812). "Seventy-five Sermons on Various Important Subjects: In this Complete Collection is Included the Eighteen Sermons Taken in Short Hand by Mr. Gurney. And to which is Now Added, a Sermon of the Character, Preaching, &c. of the Rev. Mr. Whitefield," p.158.*

[7] 2 Corinthians 10:5.

[8] Ephesians 5:22–33 is a great synopsis of the God-ordained relationship between husband and wife.

[9] Llyod-Jones, D. Martyn. *Studies in the Sermon on the Mount.* Grand Rapids, Michigan: Wm. B. Eerdmans Publishing Company, 1976. p. 428.

[10] John 9:2.

[11] As a side note and word of advice, men and women who are not married to one another should never have these conversations (or any secluded conversation) alone with the opposite sex. In these and other rare exceptions, it would be wise to skip this part in number, but absolutely maintain the spirit of seclusion and utmost privacy with one other witness.

[12] Matthew 9:1–8.

[13] http://www.foxnews.com/us/neighbor-black-man-minneapolis-shot-police-berates-protesters-this-is-not-ok.

[14] Erickson, Millard J. *Christian Theology.* Grand Rapids, Michigan: Baker Academic, 2007. P. 206.

[15] Tozer, A.W. *The Knowledge of the Holy.* San Francisco, CA: HarperSanFrancisco, 1961. P. 97.

[16] Luke 8:19–21.

[17] Obviously, there are instances when we've made a less-than-stellar choice that we must now abide by…like marrying an unbelieving spouse. In cases in which the recipient of our love does not share our love for God, yet we are "stuck" with them, we love them anyway. We pray for them, invest in them, listen, and exude the best example of 1 Corinthians 13 love possible—all in an effort to draw them to Christ.

[18] 1 John 4:19.

[19] https://ncadv.org/STATISTICS.

[20]

https://assets.speakcdn.com/assets/2497/domestic_violence_and_psychological_abuse_ncadv.pdf.

[21] https://www.rainn.org/statistics/scope-problem.

[22] https://www.childhelp.org/child-abuse-statistics/.

[23] Judges 2:14.

[24] Isaiah 1:5–6.

[25] James 4:4.

[26] Carson, D.A. *The Gospel According to John.* Grand Rapids, MI: Wm. B. Eerdmans Publishing Company, 1991. p.597.

[27] Ibid, 597.

[28] Matthew 27:46; Mark 15:34.

[29] *Thomas Sowell: Common Sense in a Senseless World. The Sowell Film.* Free to Choose Media, 2021. Accessed January 31, 2022. www.sowellfilm.com.

[30] "Interaction Institute for Social Change | Artist: Angus Maguire."

[31] The Oxford Dictionary, "Equality."

[32] http://www.humanrightscareers.com/issues/what-does-social-justice-mean/.

[33] So many resources exist to validate and expand upon these points, but a good place to begin is with the book *Black Slaveowners* by Larry Koger.

[34] Spurgeon, Charles H. *Morning and Evening.* Edited by Alistair Begg, Crossway, 2003. P. "January 17th, Morning."

[35] http://www.teenvogue.com/story/black-power-naps-addressing-systemic-racism-in-sleep.

[36] Baucham, Voddie Jr. *Fault Lines.* Washington D.C.: Salem Books, 2021. P. 69.

[37] Darrell B. Harrison, "Just Thinking Podcast" Episode #67, "Whiteness." April 14, 2019.

[38] Baucham, Voddie Jr. *Fault Lines.* P. 72.

[39] Ibid. P. 74.

[40] Ibid. P. 76.

[41] Ibid. P. 77.

[42] Ibid. P. 79.

[43] *Fault Lines* by Voddie Baucham Jr., *Wealth, Poverty, and Politics* and *Discrimination and Disparities* by Thomas Sowell, *Law,*

Legislation, and Liberty, Volume 2: The Mirage of Social Justice by
Friedrich A. Hayek are just a handful of excellent resources.

[44] 1 Peter 2:11.

[45] This is why we are supposed to proclaim the gospel to the
nations—trying to reach every people group, nation, and tribe
with the good news of Jesus Christ. He has miraculously provided
countless introductions around the globe throughout history; but
the work is not done. We must carry it out!

[46] Philo of Alexandria, a first century Jewish philosopher argued
for this point. Jones, Beth Felker, and Jeffrey W. Barbeau. *The
Image of God in an Image Driven Age: Explorations in Theological
Anthropology.* InterVarsity Press, 2016. P. 30.

[47] Jones, Beth, and Jeffrey W. Barbeau. *The Image of God in an
Image Driven Age.* P. 30.

[48] Ibid, p. 32–33.

[49] Ibid, p. 33.

[50] Ibid, p. 35–38.

[51] Ibid, p. 35–38 This argument is derived from Genesis 9:5–6,
which addresses the reasoning behind capital punishment:

> Surely I will require your lifeblood; from every beast I
> will require it. And from every man, from every man's
> brother I will require the life of a man. Whoever sheds
> man's blood, by man his blood shall be shed; for in the
> image of God He made man.

In the Old Testament, if a murder occurred, the victim's family
was to avenge their blood by taking the life of the murderer. This

practice was called being the "kinsman redeemer." While Scripture never explicitly refers to God with that term, the concept is referenced. The argument, then, is that "as the divine blood avenger, the Lord may rightly take the life of the offender, whether he does so directly through divine judgment or through an appointed human agent," because He's humanity's closest kin (Jones & Barbeau). He created us to be His family, and when we accept Christ, we do become His sons and daughters.

[52] Drew, Chris. "81 Types of Genders & Gender Identities (A to Z List)." *Helpful Professor*, 27 Nov. 2022, https://helpfulprofessor.com/types-of-genders-list/.

[53] Eunuchs were men in ancient times who qualified under one of two categories: royal servants/leaders, and castrated men who served special servant duties, particularly among the royal harem. (David Mark Rathel, "Eunuch," ed. John D. Barry et al., *The Lexham Bible Dictionary* (Bellingham, WA: Lexham Press, 2016). Castrated men serving as eunuchs obviously experienced genital mutilation; however, this was not done for gender ideology purposes.

[54] Genesis 1:24, Mark 10:2–12

[55] I say "at least" because many more can be mentioned, depending on how specific you want to get with this study.

[56] "Sex and Gender: Meanings, Definition, Identity, and Expression." *Medical News Today*, MediLexicon International, http://www.medicalnewstoday.com/articles/232363.

[57] Downes-Le Guin, Isabel. "Explaining and Treating Gender Dysphoria." *Study.com*, https://study.com/academy/lesson/explaining-and-treating-gender-identity-disorder.html.

[58] Reports, Special. "Number of Transgender Children Seeking Treatment Surges in U.S." *Reuters*, Thomson Reuters, 6 Oct. 2022, http://www.reuters.com/investigates/special-report/usa-transyouth-data/.

[59] Reports, Special. "Number of Transgender Children Seeking Treatment Surges in U.S." *Reuters*, Thomson Reuters, 6 Oct. 2022, http://www.reuters.com/investigates/special-report/usa-transyouth-data/.

[60] James Reinl, Social Affairs Correspondent. "De-Transitioners Warn of Growing Levels of Online Vitriol, Doxxing, Harassment and Death Threats." *Daily Mail Online*, Associated Newspapers, 15 Nov. 2022, http://www.dailymail.co.uk/news/article-11417609/De-transitioners-warn-growing-levels-online-vitriol-doxxing-harassment-death-threats.html?ito=social-twitter_mailonline.

[61] The Westminster Shorter Catechism states, "Man's chief end is to glorify God and to enjoy Him forever."

[62] Erickson. *Christian Theology*. P. 756–775.

[63] Colossians 1:15–21.

[64] Edwards, James R. *The Gospel According to Luke*. PNTC. P. 82.

[65] Psalm 119:105; Proverbs 4:18.

[66] Matthew 4:3.

[67] Matthew 4:4.

[68] John 6:27.

[69] John 1:14.

[70] 1 Peter 5:8.

[71] Romans 8:36b.

[72] Romans 8:34.

[73] Spurgeon, Charles H. *Morning and Evening*. Edited by Alistair Begg, Crossway, 2003. P. "January 11th, Evening."

[74] Family/Bride of Christ, New Creation, Set Apart, Salt and Light, His Workmanship, Servants, Ministers of the Gospel, Disciples, Filled with the Spirit—Spiritual Gifts and Abilities, Loved, Secure, His Hands, Feet, Heart, and Voice in the World…just to name a few.

[75] Spurgeon, Charles H. *Morning and Evening*. Edited by Alistair Begg, Crossway, 2003. P. "January 18th, Evening."

www.ingramcontent.com/pod-product-compliance
Lightning Source LLC
Chambersburg PA
CBHW071417090426
42737CB00011B/1493